labrese Sopressata Camembert Capicola Cheddar C

Fog Manchego Mimolette Mozzarella P'tit Basq Parmigiano Reggiano Pecor

pressata Stilton Swiss Taleggio Truffle Salami Wensleydale Alp Blossom Applew

ert Capicola Cheddar Chorizo Feta Fromager d'Affinois Genoa Salami Germ

Mimolette Mozzarella P'tit Basqu Parmigiano Reggiano Pecorino Romano Pep

Swiss Taleggio Truffle Salami Wensleydale Alp Blossom Applewood Smoked Sal

dar Chorizo Feta Fromager d'Affinois Genoa Salami German Sausage Gorgonz

P'tit Basqu Parmigiano Reggiano Pecorino Romano Pepper Jack Pepperoni Po

fle Salami Wensleydale Alp Blossom Applewood Smoked Salami Asiago Bresa

Fromager d'Affinois Genoa Salami German Sausage Gorgonzola Gouda Hallou

giano Reggiano Pecorino Romano Pepper Jack Pepperoni Port Salut Prosciu

eydale Alp Blossom Applewood Smoked Salami Asiago Bresaola Brie Bour

Affinois Genoa Salami German Sausage Gorgonzola Gouda Halloumi Harbi

Around the Board

DK

Around the Board

BOARDS · PLATTERS · PLATES

EMILY DELANEY

Publisher Mike Sanders
Senior Editor Alexandra Andrzejewski
Assistant Director of Art/Design Rebecca Batchelor
Photographer Daniel Showalter
Food Stylist Emily Delaney
Chef Ashley Brooks
Proofreaders Lisa Starnes, Amy J. Schneider
Indexer Celia McCoy

First American Edition, 2022
Published in the United States by DK Publishing
6081 E. 82nd Street, Indianapolis, IN 46250

Library of Congress Catalog Number: 2021943695
ISBN: 978-0-7440-4570-3

Note: This publication contains the opinions and ideas of its author. It is intended
to provide helpful and informative material on the subject matter covered. It is sold with
the understanding that the author and publisher are not engaged in rendering
professional services in the book. If the reader requires personal assistance or advice,
a competent professional should be consulted. The author and publisher specifically
disclaim any responsibility for any liability, loss, or risk, personal or otherwise, which is
incurred as a consequence, directly or indirectly, of the use and application of any of the
contents of this book.

Trademarks: All terms mentioned in this book that are known to be or are suspected of being
trademarks or service marks have been appropriately capitalized. Alpha Books, DK, and
Penguin Random House LLC cannot attest to the accuracy of this information. Use of a term in
this book should not be regarded as affecting the validity of any trademark or service mark.

DK books are available at special discounts when purchased in bulk for sales promotions,
premiums, fund-raising, or educational use. For details, contact: SpecialSales@dk.com

Printed and bound in China

Photographs on pages 8, 13, and 192 by Paige Babilla Photography
Photographs on pages 46, 48, 148, and 149 © Cheese Board Queen LLC

All other images © Dorling Kindersley Limited

For the curious
www.dk.com

For my parents, who make every dream possible.

Contents

The Art of the Board

Winter

Spring

Summer

Fall

Author's Introduction

On a chilly night in November a few years ago, I walked into a friend's apartment carrying a cheese board. It was the item I'd been assigned to bring for our annual Friendsgiving gathering, and while the assignment was not random—my penchant for making boards was well known by then—I had never made one quite like this before. Nearly two feet in diameter and filled to the brim with an array of fall colors and flavors, it was a thing of beauty and the very definition of bountiful.

I had lugged my hefty masterpiece halfway across the city, balancing it ever so carefully on my lap in the back of an Uber and carrying it up three flights of stairs before arriving at the door of our hostess's third floor apartment. What happened next is nothing short of magic, and the reason I'm sharing this story with you today.

As I stepped into that tiny living room filled with 14 lively guests and at least 2 dogs, suddenly you could hear a pin drop. Everyone stopped in their tracks and rushed to get a closer look at the beautiful arrangement of delicious cheeses, meats, and accoutrements before digging in. And then? They stayed there—gathered around the board enjoying good food and even better conversation.

I am constantly inspired by the magic of that moment, and it's been the spark behind Cheese Board Queen, a community built around my passion for bringing people together around beautiful boards and taking the guesswork out of making them.

Within these pages I've written down my favorite recipes of boards to enjoy throughout the year, from holidays and special occasions to ordinary weeknights that call for something special. Along the way, I share my tips for everything from selecting the best ingredients to styling a beautiful arrangement so that you can confidently create your own magical moments gathered around a board unlike any you've made before.

Emily Delaney
The Cheese Board Queen

The Art of the Board

Gather Around

Within this chapter, you'll find everything you need to know about the art of the board, from a crash course on key ingredients to the principles of styling and pairing ingredients. You'll build a foundation of knowledge and skills that will help you confidently create any of the nearly 50 boards included in the next four chapters. Gather around and let's begin!

THE CHEESE BOARD QUEEN PHILOSOPHY

I believe that the art of the board should be approachable, accessible, and personal. That the time spent gathered around a board is more important than the time spent making it—although making it should be fun, too!

The true magic of a board lies in the understanding that it is so much more than the sum of its parts. It's a chance to create something special to share with family and friends. It's the world's best ice breaker for a room full of friends who haven't met yet, and it's a beautiful way to explore and appreciate the vast culinary world.

A WORD ON INGREDIENTS

A board is not only a beauty to behold, but also a culinary adventure that puts a spotlight on the ingredients.

The process of creating a delicious board begins at the grocery store as you select cheeses with different textures and milk types (we'll dive into this on page 16) and fill your cart with a variety of meats, fruit, crackers, and other items.

While quality is important and some ingredients are better suited for boards than others, you should feel empowered to think outside the box and choose the ingredients that you love. That said, I encourage you to always be intentional with the flavors you include and to step outside your comfort zone and try at least one new-to-you cheese, meat, or accoutrement on each board you make. Not sure where to begin? Ask your cheesemonger (they're the knowledgeable experts behind the cheese counter) for their recommendations. And when all else fails, let the flavors of the season inspire and guide you.

BOARDS FOR ALL SEASONS & ALL OCCASIONS

From holidays to birthdays and everything in between, there are countless opportunities to gather and celebrate throughout the year. A board is the perfect addition to the menu for any occasion for a variety of reasons:

- It's a one-and-done appetizer that can be made in advance and doesn't require cooking.
- It's a fun and easy way to incorporate a theme.
- It's a guaranteed crowd-pleaser.

In addition to a specific holiday or theme, I'm always inspired by the flavors and colors of the seasons and find them to be a helpful guide when it comes to selecting ingredients for a board.

The chapters in this book are organized by season, taking you around the year with ideas and recipes for dozens of boards that are inspired by both the occasions that fill our calendars and the items that line our pantries.

Principles of Pairing

The appeal of the "grazing" style of dining can largely be attributed to the way it invites creativity to the way we eat. A board filled with a variety of flavors and textures is an opportunity to revisit favorite pairings and discover new combinations. When it comes to choosing the right balance of flavors and building those perfect bites, there are a few helpful principles to keep in mind.

THE PERFECT MATCH

The most straightforward way to approach flavor pairings is to identify flavors that complement—or match—one another. Pairing sweet with sweet and savory with savory creates a balanced bite that enhances the flavors of each item.

Try pairing a vintage English cheddar with a slice of apple and a drizzle of honey, and notice how the combination amps up the sweetness of the cheddar and the floral notes of the honey.

This principle applies to texture, too. A piece of soft, creamy Brie with a drizzle of honey or a ripe raspberry feels luxurious on the palate while a bite of aged Gouda with a crunchy cracker creates a heartier effect.

OPPOSITES ATTRACT

It may sound counterintuitive, but contrasting flavors can actually create harmony and balance. Think about some of your favorite dishes that combine sweet and savory flavors (looking at you, maple bacon donuts) and how that contrast makes for a more interesting, flavorful bite.

In some cases, contrast is a great way to mellow out strong flavors and make them more palatable. A classic example of this is a drizzle of honey on a piece of funky blue cheese. In other cases,

contrast is used to enhance flavors and transform them into something completely new and exciting. One of my favorite examples of this approach is the addictingly tangy-sweet combination of goat cheese with fresh figs and balsamic glaze.

Once again, texture is just as important as flavor, so consider combining creamy cheeses with crunchy crackers, or hard cheeses with jam, and notice how the contrast creates a party on your palate that you just can't get enough of.

WHAT GROWS TOGETHER, GOES TOGETHER

A classic and nearly foolproof approach to pairing is to consider where and when the food is made or grown. The idea behind this approach is that foods with shared terroir (or land), cultural influences, production methods, and even growing seasons are likely to pair together.

To put this principle into practice, try creating a board filled with Italian cheeses, meats, and antipasto items; or try any of the seasonal pairings boards in this book for a tasting experience centered around seasonal flavors.

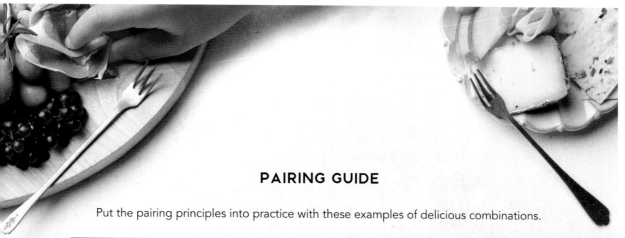

PAIRING GUIDE

Put the pairing principles into practice with these examples of delicious combinations.

CHEESE	FLAVOR & TEXTURE NOTES	COMPLEMENTARY PAIRINGS	CONTRASTING PAIRINGS
Fresh goat cheese	Bright, tangy, acidic; soft, creamy	Olives Citrus Cherries Prosciutto	Fresh berries Honey Dried apricots Crunchy crackers
Brie	Buttery, mild, notes of mushroom; creamy, smooth, decadent	Honey Figs Fresh berries Prosciutto	Cornichons Apples and pears Nuts Crusty bread
Blue cheese	Funky, sharp, salty; creamy, a bit crumbly	Olives Cornichons Salami	Honey Dried fruit Dark chocolate Nuts
Aged cheddar	Nutty, sharp, mildly sweet, slightly earthy; firm but crumbly, slightly crunchy	Jam Apples Grapes Crunchy crackers	Grainy mustard Cornichons Salami Nuts
Gouda	Nutty, salty, notes of caramel; firm but smooth, sometimes with a slight crunch	Salami Crunchy crackers Nuts	Fig jam Apples and pears Olives Dried fruit Dark chocolate

Cheese

The world of cheese is vast, spanning centuries of tradition from every corner of the globe. The seemingly endless variety is exciting and delicious to explore, but it can also be overwhelming. Luckily, there are some commonly defined categories that make it easier to navigate the cheese case.

CATEGORIES OF CHEESE

FRESH

Fresh cheeses are intended to be eaten immediately after they're made, while they're still fresh! Because they're not aged, fresh cheeses have a high moisture content that makes them soft and spreadable and gives them a mild, milky flavor.

Examples: Fresh mozzarella, fresh goat cheese, mascarpone

BLOOMY RIND

These cheeses develop soft, white, edible rinds as they ripen, thanks to the addition of friendly molds like penicillium candidum. These rinds help create soft, buttery textures that develop further as the cheeses mature from the outside in.

Examples: Brie, Camembert

BLUE

The ones everyone loves to hate. The classic blue veins are the result of blue mold spores added to the milk that grow with the help of oxygen as the cheeses mature. Blue cheeses are known for their distinct smells and sharp, salty flavors.

Examples: Stilton, Gorgonzola, Roquefort

SEMIHARD

As cheese ages, it loses moisture and develops deeper flavor. Semihard cheeses strike a balance between the buttery, creamy notes of younger cheeses and the nutty, salty notes of aged cheeses.

Examples: Gouda, cheddar, havarti, Gruyère

HARD

Hard cheeses have been aged the longest and have little to no moisture left. They boast complex depths of flavors, usually with notes of browned butter or nuts, and firm, crumbly textures.

Examples: Parmigiano-Reggiano, Pecorino Romano

WASHED RIND

These cheeses are treated with brine or other mold-bearing agents. This encourages the growth of bacteria on their rinds, giving them their unique orange hues, funky smells, and distinct flavors that are often more mild than their smells would suggest.

Examples: Taleggio, Limburger, Époisses

TYPES OF MILK

COW

Cow's milk is perhaps the most commonly used. With a mildly earthy, buttery flavor profile, it's the foundation for some of the world's most popular cheeses, from Brie to cheddar.

GOAT

The diet of goats and the unique composition of fatty acids in their milk results in cheeses that are bright and tangy with earthier, grassier notes than those made with cow's milk.

SHEEP

Sheep's milk is high in fat, making it ideal for cheese-making. In fact, it's used almost exclusively to make cheeses like feta, Manchego, Pecorino Romano, and Roquefort.

Parmigiano-Reggiano

Brie

Taleggio

Blue Cheese

Goat Cheese

Gouda

Charcuterie & Salume

Perhaps equally important as the cheeses you select are the meats chosen to accompany them, and luckily there is a wide variety to choose from. Historically speaking, *salume* is the Italian term for salted and cured uncooked meats like salami and prosciutto while *charcuterie* is the French term for preparing cooked meats like pâté. Today, the words are often used interchangeably to describe the cured meats often added to antipasto platters and cheese boards.

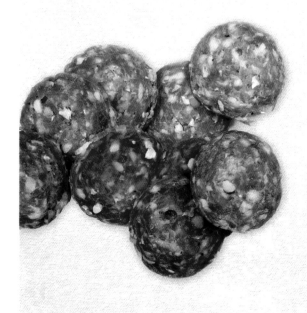

Salami

The word *salami* is derived from the Italian word "salume," which broadly refers to the many types of salted and cured meats that have been made as a method for preserving meat for more than 2,000 years.

Salami itself is a category of Italian cured sausages, typically made with ground pork that's mixed with a variety of seasonings before being stuffed into natural casings and hung to dry—or cure—for weeks, months, or years. There are many types of salami, each defined by where and how they are made. Common varieties include Genoa, sopressata, pepperoni, chorizo, and those flavored with spices like fennel (finocchiona), black pepper, and even red wine.

Prosciutto

Prosciutto is the Italian word for "ham," and prosciutto crudo is the uncooked, dry-cured ham that is often served on charcuterie boards. To make prosciutto, pork legs are generously coated in salt by a *maestro salatore* (salt master) and left to dry—or cure—for several weeks. This process not only makes the uncooked meat safe to eat but also gives it its concentrated flavor. The cured pork legs are washed, seasoned, and dry aged for up to three years. When it's ready to enjoy, prosciutto is shaved into paper-thin slices with a buttery texture that melts in the mouth and a delicious salty-sweet flavor that pairs with a variety of cheeses and accoutrements.

Capicola

Capicola, also known as capocollo or coppa, is a traditional Italian dry-cured pork charcuterie made from the coppa muscle, which runs along the neck and shoulders. Capicola is seasoned with red wine, garlic, and a variety of herbs and spices before it's salted, stuffed in a natural casing, and hung to cure for up to 6 months. With a ratio of 30 percent fat to 70 percent lean, capicola is moist and tender and boasts rich flavor that makes it the perfect addition to sandwiches, pizzas, and boards filled with a variety of cheeses and antipasto items.

Bresaola

Bresaola is an air-dried beef charcuterie with origins in northern Italy's Lombardy region. The traditional method of meticulously trimming the fat from the beef results in a much leaner meat than prosciutto and other salumi. When the meat is trimmed, it's cured with salt and spices like juniper, cinnamon, clove, garlic, and citrus, and dredged through red wine before being aged for several weeks.

Like most charcuterie, bresaola should be sliced paper-thin for serving. The lean texture and complex beef flavor make it a delicious pairing with aged Italian cheeses, olives, and nuts.

Principles of Styling

The key to an eye-catching, show-stopping board is all about the creative arrangement of naturally beautiful ingredients. My approach to styling includes four key principles that can be applied to any combination of ingredients and will result in a stunning presentation every time.

VARIETY

This styling principle is as much about the ingredients you choose as it is about the way you arrange them on the board.

Showcase the variety of your ingredients by placing cheeses and meats in separate areas, breaking up items with similar shapes and sizes, and applying the styling principles of texture and color to create pockets of visual interest. The end result will be a varied yet cohesive display that draws the eye around the board.

TEXTURE

Many of the core elements of a board are actually quite flat—from the cheese and charcuterie, to the crackers and even the board itself.

Presented as-is, straight out of their packaging, these elements would make for a very one-dimensional board. But a few simple styling tricks like slicing the cheeses, folding the charcuterie, and layering the crackers will add texture that literally elevates the ingredients.

Additional opportunities to create texture include adding small vessels of jam and honey, building piles of produce, filling in open spaces with nuts, and garnishing with sprigs of fresh herbs.

COLOR

Incorporating color is the easiest way to create visual interest for a truly show-stopping board. As you flip through the pages in this book, notice how I use fresh produce, jam, honey, and other accoutrements to create a cohesive color palette that enhances the neutral colors of cheese, crackers, and charcuterie.

THEME

A board is a creative way to incorporate the theme of a gathering into the menu. The sky is the limit, so feel free to think outside the box as you work to bring the theme to life through the colors, flavors, and shapes of the ingredients you choose.

SERVING SIZES

Cheese: A good rule of thumb is to serve 2 oz (55g) of cheese per guest. So, if you are hosting 3 friends, you will want 2–3 cheeses weighing 6 oz (170g, or around ⅓ lb) total.

Charcuterie: Similarly, I recommend serving 2–3 oz (55–85g) of charcuterie per guest. A 4 oz (110g) package of presliced prosciutto and an 8 oz (225g) log of hard salami will do the trick for a group of 4 to 6.

Adjust quantities as needed to suit the appetite of your guests and the role of the board on your menu—is it an appetizer or the main dish?

HOW TO SLICE CHEESE

- **Blocks:** Lay the cheese flat on a cutting board. Use a sharp kitchen knife or cheese knife to remove any rinds, if desired, and cut even slices along the long side of the block, creating thin rectangular pieces about ¼ inch (.5cm) thick. Use this method for blocks of cheddar, Gruyère, and Comté.

- **Semihard wedges:** Remove any wax coating. Lay the cheese flat on a cutting board with the thin edge facing away from you and the triangular sides facing out. With a sharp kitchen knife or cheese knife, cut vertically along the triangular edge, creating long triangular pieces about ¼ inch (.5cm) thick. Use this method for wedges of Gouda and Manchego.

- **Hard wedges:** Lay the cheese flat on a cutting board. Starting at the thin tip of the wedge, use the tip of a spade knife or flat knife to chisel rustic, bite-sized pieces. Use this method for aged Gouda and Parmigiano-Reggiano.

- **Soft wedges:** Lay the cheese flat on a cutting board. Use a wire cutter or soft cheese knife to cut triangular serving-sized wedges. Use this method for blue cheeses.

- **Wheels:** Lay the wheel flat on a cutting board. Use a soft cheese knife or slim blade cheese knife to cut the wheel in half, then into quarters, and so on until you have the desired number of wedges. Use this method for wheels of Brie, Camembert, and Gouda.

- **Logs:** Lay the cheese horizontally on a cutting board. Use a wire cutter or soft cheese knife to cut the cheese into thin, even rounds about ¼ inch (.5cm) thick. Use this method for logs of chèvre.

PROSCIUTTO RIBBONS

Step 1: Carefully remove the paper backing from a slice of prosciutto and hold it lengthwise in front of you with the white, fatty edge facing out. **Tip:** For easier handling, use kitchen shears to cut the prosciutto in half lengthwise prior to removing it from the paper backing.

Step 2: Using your fingers, loosely scrunch and gather the prosciutto as you bring your hands together to meet in the middle. Place the folded prosciutto on the board with the white fatty edge facing up.

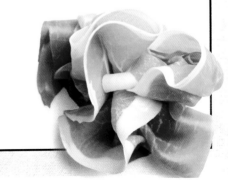

FOLDED SALAMI

Step 1: Hold a slice of salami flat in front of you.

Step 2: Fold the salami in half once, creating a half-moon shape. Use your thumbs to lightly crease the fold.

Step 3: Fold the salami in half again, bringing the corners of the half-moon together to create a wedge. Use your thumbs to lightly crease the fold. Repeat to build a stack of salami wedges and serve on the board with the creased edges facing down.

A few simple folds give charcuterie texture, dimension, and character to match its bold, delicious flavor.

Prep & Serve

While there are no required tools or supplies for making cheese boards (in fact, you likely have everything you need in your own kitchen), there are some tools that will help streamline your slicing, up your presentation, and elevate the dining experience for your guests.

TOOLS & KNIVES

HONEY DIPPER

A handy tool that makes it easy to achieve the perfect honey drizzle. Honey dippers come in a variety of sizes and materials and add a charming touch to any cheese board.

CHEESE SLICING BOARD

Practical and stylish. Use this tool to prep clean slices of soft and hard cheeses alike, or use it as a serving piece that guests can use to cut their own slices.

CHEESE KNIVES

Slim-blade knife: The barely-there blade and offset handle make it easy to cut clean, even slices of semihard and soft cheeses.

Soft cheese knife: Designed with holes along the blade to reduce the surface area and keep soft, creamy cheeses from sticking.

Spade knife: Also known as a Parmesan knife, this sharp, pointed blade is best for cutting into hard cheeses like Parmigiano-Reggiano and aged Gouda.

WIRE CUTTER

Wire is ideal for cutting soft cheeses like chèvre because it cuts through cleanly without adding pressure that can crush or break the cheese.

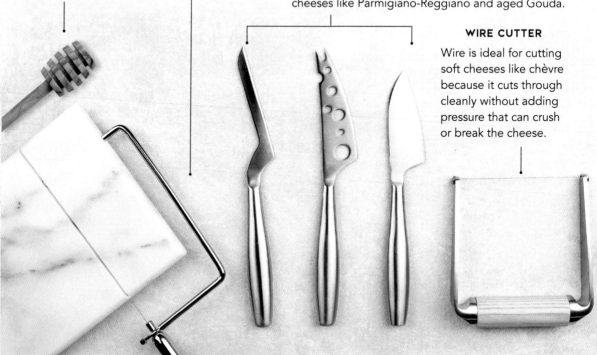

BOARDS

Materials: Wood, slate, and marble are classic cheese board materials. They're beautiful, easy to clean, and when cared for properly, they can last a lifetime. To protect your boards from stains and wear, seal wood and slate with a food-safe mineral oil, and seal marble with a food-safe marble sealer.

Shapes and sizes: From round to rectangular, personal-sized to table-length, boards come in a variety of shapes and sizes. While primarily a matter of preference, I recommend keeping the size and setting of the gathering in mind when choosing a board. For example, a 13-inch (33-cm) round board is perfect for gathering around a table with a small group, while a 14 x 18-inch (36 x 46cm) rectangular board offers more space to fill with goodies for a crowd and allows guests to spread out as they graze.

BOWLS & VESSELS

The vessels used to hold items like jam, honey, and olives are not only practical but another opportunity to add visual interest to your board. Choose decorative pinch bowls, mini jars, and ramekins in a variety of shapes, sizes, and colors. **Tip:** Keep these items small so that proportions remain balanced.

SPREADERS

Just as the name implies, these spatula-shaped knives are ideal for spreading soft, creamy cheeses onto crackers and bread.

FORK

A multipurpose tool that holds hard cheeses in place while cutting or functions as a serving utensil for picking up pieces of cheese, charcuterie, and other ingredients.

PRONGED KNIFE

Also known as a fork-tipped spear. Use this handy tool to slice through soft and semihard cheeses and serve them using the pronged tip.

FLAT KNIVES

Sometimes called chisel knives, these wide, flat blades are commonly found in cheese knife sets and can be used to cut, slice, and chisel a variety of cheeses.

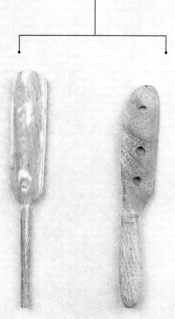

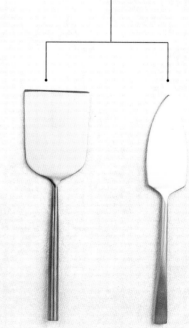

Winter

Your Winter
Pantry

In most parts of the world, the winter season is less vibrant and bountiful than the rest of the year. But while the produce section is certainly more sparse than during the summer months, what it lacks in variety it redeems ten-fold in bold colors and flavors that complement the complexity and richness of wintery cheeses and accoutrements. Here's a peek inside your winter pantry:

THE PRODUCE

Blackberries
Blood oranges
Cara cara oranges
Clementines
Cranberries
Grapefruits
Pears (Bosc, Bartlett, Red Anjou, etc.)
Pomegranates
Raspberries
Red grapes

THE CHEESES

BellaVitano
Blue cheeses (Gorgonzola Dolce, Roquefort, Bayley Hazen Blue, etc.)
Brie
Cheddar
Comté
Cranberry chèvre
Cranberry Wensleydale
Gouda
Gruyère
Harbison
Morbier
Ossau-Iraty/Esquirrou
Parmigiano-Reggiano
Pleasant Ridge Reserve
P'tit Basque
Rush Creek Reserve
Taleggio
Truffle Gouda
Truffle Tremor

THE ACCOUTREMENTS

Cornichons
Cranberry jam
Cranberry-orange jam
Crusty bread
Dark chocolate
Dried apricots
Dried citrus
Dried figs
Fig jam
Fruit and nut crisps
Grainy mustard
Marcona almonds
Mixed roasted nuts
Olives
Orange jam/marmalade
Raspberry jam
Rustic crackers
Sour cherry jam
Spiced cherry jam

WINTER PAIRINGS BOARD

As a Midwesterner, I have a—well—*complicated* relationship with winter. When I can look past the freezing temperatures and lack of sunshine, I find there is actually a lot of beauty in winter—from the bold, rich flavors of the foods we enjoy to the bright pops of color from a juicy pomegranate or zesty orange. This board is a celebration of those beautiful winter moments, and while most of the boards in this chapter are tied to a specific winter holiday or special occasion, this is one to save for a dreary, snowy day when you're craving a special meal or an impromptu gathering with friends or family.

Shopping List

CHEESE
Aged Gouda
Blue cheese
Esquirrou
Harbison

MEAT
Capicola
Hard salami

PRODUCE
Pears (mix of Bosc and
  Red Anjou)
Pomegranate
Red grapes
Rosemary
Thyme

CRUNCH
Crusty bread
Fig and olive crisps
Flatbread crackers
Mixed nuts

ACCOUTREMENTS
Cornichons
Fig jam
Grainy mustard
Honey
Olives

BUILD IT

Prep: Wash and dry all produce. Cut the Esquirrou into thin triangular slices. Use the tip of a knife to break off bite-sized pieces of Gouda. Slice off the top rind of the Harbison. Thinly slice the salami. Thinly slice the pears. Cut the pomegranate into small segments. Add the jam, mustard, and honey to small bowls.

Build: Arrange the **Esquirrou (1), Harbison (2), aged Gouda (3),** and **blue cheese (4)** near the edges of the board. Place the bowls of **jam (5), mustard (6),** and **honey (7).** Add a few bunches of **grapes (8),** stacks of **pear slices (9),** and segments of **pomegranate (10).** Build small piles of **olives (11)** and **cornichons (12).**

Fold the **capicola (13)** and tuck it into an open space. Neatly arrange the sliced **salami (14).** Add piles of **crackers (15), bread (16),** and **crisps (17).** Fill in any gaps with **mixed nuts (18).** Garnish with **rosemary** and **thyme (19).**

Serve: Enjoy immediately or cover and refrigerate until 20 to 30 minutes before serving.

Bright, seasonal produce complements an array of complex, rich cheeses and savory accoutrements.

PAIRINGS	A little bit of this, a little bit of that. With a range of sweet, savory, and slightly funky flavors, this board offers endless opportunities to create perfectly balanced, flavorful bites. Here are a few of my favorite combinations.

HARBISON

Crusty bread
Cornichons
Grainy
    mustard
Pears

ESQUIRROU

Fig and olive
    crisps
Honey
Olives
Red grapes

AGED GOUDA

Fig and olive
    crisps
Fig jam
Pomegranate
Pear

BLUE CHEESE

Flatbread crackers
Honey
Pomegranate
Red grapes

HOLIDAY HOSTING BOARD

The holiday season is chock-full of opportunities to let your inner host shine, whether you're arranging a gift exchange, throwing a festive soiree with friends, or gathering the whole family for dinner. With a list of straightforward ingredients that come together with a bit of styling and a touch of holiday sparkle from sugared cranberries and rosemary, this board is a host's secret to stress-free entertaining.

Shopping List

CHEESE

Brie

Cranberry chèvre (page 49, or store-bought)

Goat milk Gouda (such as Cypress Grove's Midnight Moon)

MEAT

Prosciutto

Sopressata

PRODUCE

Sugared Cranberries & Rosemary (page 37)

Bosc pears

Pomegranate

Red grapes

CRUNCH

Cranberry-hazelnut crisps

Flatbread crackers

Marcona almonds

ACCOUTREMENTS

Castelvetrano olives

Cranberry-orange jam

Dried citrus

Dried figs

Honey

BUILD IT

Prep: Make the Sugared Cranberries & Rosemary (page 37) up to 2 days in advance. Wash and dry all produce. Cut the goat milk Gouda into thin, triangular slices. Slice a few rounds of the cranberry chèvre. Thinly slice the pears. Cut the pomegranate into small segments. Add the jam, honey, and olives to small bowls.

Build: Arrange the **goat milk Gouda (1)**, **Brie (2)**, and **cranberry chèvre (3)** near the edges of the board. Place the bowls of **jam (4)**, **honey (5)**, and **olives (6)**. Place bunches of **grapes (7)**, stacks of **pear slices (8)**, and segments of **pomegranate (9)**. Add at least two sections of each produce element for visual interest.

Fold the **prosciutto (10)** and **sopressata (11)**, and tuck them into open spaces on the board. Create stacked and fanned arrangements of **crackers (12)** and **crisps (13)**. Fill in any gaps with **marcona almonds (14)**. Garnish with **dried fruit (15)** and **Sugared Cranberries & Rosemary (16)**.

Serve: Enjoy immediately or cover and refrigerate until 20 to 30 minutes before serving. Serve with a bold, fruit-forward red or crisp, bubbly Prosecco.

SUGARED CRANBERRIES & ROSEMARY

These sugar-frosted garnishes come together in a snap and add elevated, festive flair to your holiday boards. The cranberries sweeten in the simple syrup, so they taste as good as they look!

MAKES: about 1½ cups cranberries and .75 oz (21g) rosemary

TOTAL TIME: 45 minutes, plus 2 hours for cooling

---

12 oz (340g) fresh cranberries

2 cups cane sugar, divided

½ cup water or orange juice

Zest of ½ orange (optional)

1 pkg (about .75 oz/21g) rosemary

TIP: Use as a garnish for cheese boards, cocktails, and desserts.

1. Wash and dry the cranberries. Line a baking sheet with parchment paper.

2. In a small saucepan, combine ½ cup sugar, the water or orange juice, and orange zest (if using).

3. Stir over medium-low heat until the sugar is dissolved. Simmer gently for 1 minute (but do not boil). Remove from the heat and cool for 5 minutes.

4. In small batches, add the cranberries and gently stir until evenly coated. Soak for at least 5 minutes or up to overnight.

5. Remove the cranberries with a slotted spoon and transfer to the prepared baking sheet. Repeat with the rosemary. Allow to dry for 1 hour, or until dry and still slightly sticky to touch.

6. Fill a small bowl with the remaining 1½ cups sugar. Gently roll or toss the cranberries and rosemary to coat. Return to the lined baking sheet to dry for 1 hour.

7. Store in an airtight container and refrigerate. If needed, toss in more sugar before serving.

An elevated, festive color palette comes to life with sugar-frosted cranberries and rosemary that sparkle like the snow falling outside.

CHRISTMAS BRIE BOARD

Nothing warms the soul quite like warm, melty baked Brie. This version gets the holiday treatment with the addition of a sweet cranberry compote topping before it's wrapped up like a Christmas present in puff pastry. It's perfect on its own (served with crusty baguette, of course), but add it to a board or platter arranged with a variety of crackers, a couple of cheeses, and a handful of accoutrements, and it becomes the star of a show-stopping, all-in-one holiday appetizer.

Shopping List

CHEESE
Holiday Baked Brie
 (page 41)
Cranberry Wensleydale
White cheddar (such as
 Milton Creamery's Prairie
 Breeze or Barber's 1833)

PRODUCE
Sugared Cranberries
 (page 37)
Pomegranate
Raspberries
Red grapes
Rosemary

ACCOUTREMENTS
Dried citrus
Dried cranberries
Honey
Spiced cherry jam

MEAT
Prosciutto

CRUNCH
Baguette
Cinnamon cookies or
 crackers
Cranberry-hazelnut crisps
Marcona almonds or
 candied pecans

BUILD IT

Prep: Prepare the Holiday Baked Brie (page 41). Wash and dry all produce. Cut the pomegranate into small segments. Use the tip of a knife to break off bite-sized pieces of cheddar. Add the jam and honey to small bowls.

Build: Arrange the **cheddar (1)** and **cranberry Wensleydale (2)** near the edges of the board, saving space for the baked Brie. Place the bowls of **jam (3)** and **honey (4).**

Fold the **prosciutto (5)** and tuck it into an open space. Arrange the **baguette (6), crisps (7),** and **cookies or crackers (8).** Add 2 to 3 bunches of **grapes (9)** and piles of **raspberries (10).** Fill in any gaps with **marcona almonds (11)** and segments of **pomegranate (12).** Once cooled, add the **Holiday Baked Brie (13)** to the reserved space. Garnish with **Sugared Cranberries (14), dried fruit (15),** and **rosemary (16).**

Serve: Enjoy immediately.

HOLIDAY BAKED BRIE

A simple cranberry compote, honey, and crunchy pecans add a touch of sweetness to the savory, buttery flavor of melted Brie wrapped inside golden puff pastry.

MAKES: 6 servings

TOTAL TIME: 45 minutes, plus cooling

---

1 sheet of frozen puff pastry

1 cup fresh cranberries

½ cup cranberry juice

2 tbsp honey, plus more to drizzle

2 sprigs of fresh rosemary

3–4 sprigs of fresh thyme

2 tsp fresh lemon juice

½ tsp lemon zest

8 oz (225g) wheel of Brie

¼ cup chopped pecans

1 large egg

1 tbsp water

---

1. Line a baking sheet with parchment paper. Remove the puff pastry from the freezer and thaw according to the package instructions.

2. In a small saucepan, combine the cranberries, cranberry juice, and honey. Stir over medium-high heat, and bring to a low boil. Lower the heat and simmer.

3. Add the rosemary, thyme, lemon juice, and lemon zest. Simmer for 8 to 10 minutes, or until the cranberries have popped. Taste and adjust sweetness with more honey if needed.

4. Discard the rosemary and thyme sprigs. Transfer the mixture to a bowl to cool.

5. Meanwhile, on a clean, floured work surface, use a rolling pin to roll out the thawed puff pastry until it's about ⅛ inch (3mm) thick.

6. Place the Brie in the center of the puff pastry. Spread a thin layer of the cooled cranberry mixture on top of the Brie. Top with the chopped pecans and a light drizzle of honey.

7. Preheat the oven to 375°F (180°C). In a small bowl, whisk together the egg and water. Brush the perimeter of the puff pastry with the egg wash. Fold the pastry up and over the Brie toward the center. Press gently to seal, and use a knife to trim off any excess dough. If you'd like, use a cookie cutter to create star or snowflake shapes with the excess dough, and place them on top of the wrapped Brie.

8. Transfer the wrapped Brie to the prepared baking sheet. Brush the top and sides with the egg wash. For best results, place in the freezer for 30 minutes or up to 1 hour before baking.

9. Bake for 30 to 35 minutes, rotating the sheet halfway through, until the pastry is puffy and golden brown. If you added cutout decorations, cover them with a small piece of aluminum foil when you rotate to prevent them from overbrowning. Remove from the oven and let cool for 10 minutes. Transfer the warm baked Brie to your board.

ANTIPASTO CHARCUTEWREATH

A stunning centerpiece and delicious appetizer all in one, the charcutewreath is an easy way to add some holiday magic to your table. The sky is the limit when it comes to choosing the ingredients and design of these edible wreaths—they can be sweet or savory, elaborate or simple, big or small. This antipasto version features a variety of delicious Italian cheeses, meats, and my favorite items from the olive bar, including olives, artichokes, and peppers, all arranged on a bed of fresh rosemary.

Shopping List

CHEESE

Brie (4 oz/110g wheel)

Gorgonzola

Mini or bite-sized fresh mozzarella (often called ciliegine)

MEAT

Capicola

Sopressata

PRODUCE

Rosemary (about 3 oz/85g)

Other fresh herbs or greenery (optional)

Sugared Cranberries (optional; page 37)

CRUNCH

Baguette or Italian bread

Marcona almonds

Shelled pistachios

ANTIPASTO

Marinated artichokes

Olives (2–3 types)

Peppadew peppers

Other antipasto items of choice (optional)

BUILD IT

Prep: Wash and dry all herbs and greens. Slice the baguette.

Build: On a round board, build the foundation of your wreath by placing 3 to 4 small bowls around the perimeter. Densely arrange the **rosemary and other herbs or greenery (1)** between the bowls all around the perimeter of the board. Add the **artichokes (2), olives (3), peppers (4),** and any other antipasto items to the small bowls. Place the **Brie (5)** and **Gorgonzola (6),** and create 3 to 4 small piles of **mozzarella (7).** Fold and stack the **sopressata (8)** and **capicola (9),** and arrange in small sections on the board. Add small stacks of **baguette (10)** and piles of **marcona almonds (11)** and **pistachios (12).** Fill in any gaps with extra rosemary and greens. Garnish with **Sugared Cranberries (13)** (if using).

Serve: Enjoy immediately or cover and refrigerate until 20 to 30 minutes before serving. Serve with extra bread on the side.

Fresh rosemary creates a beautiful, fragrant foundation that brings your wreath to life.

MORE CHARCUTEWREATH IDEAS

Whether savory or sweet, big or small, elaborate or simple, the charcutewreath is a quick and easy way to add some holiday magic to your table. Here are some other creative charcutewreath ideas to make and enjoy throughout the season.

SWEET & CHEESY

Pair your favorite holiday sweets with decadent, savory cheeses for a beautiful, delicious, and unexpected holiday dessert.

- Brie
- Cranberry Wensleydale
- Blue cheese
- Prosciutto
- Raspberries
- Honey
- Candied pecans
- Chocolate truffles
- Milk or dark chocolate
- Gingerbread cookies
- Dried citrus
- Sugared cranberries

RED & WHITE

Stick to red and white foods, such as the ones listed below, arranged in an alternating pattern to give your wreath a festive candy cane–like feel.

- Cranberry chèvre
- Mini Brie bites
- Salami
- Red berries
- Red grapes
- White chocolate–covered pretzels
- Holiday cookies
- Marcona almonds
- Sugared cranberries
- Mini candy canes

KID-FRIENDLY

Pull out the mini holiday-themed cookie cutters, and get the kiddos involved with making cutout cheese shapes and placing piles of ingredients around the board.

- Havarti
- White cheddar
- Salami
- Grapes
- Strawberries
- Raspberries
- Gingerbread cookies
- Decorated holiday cookies
- Pretzels
- Almonds

BOARD-AMENT

If only this festive board could fit on the Christmas tree! To make your own ornament-inspired board, start by selecting a color palette and pattern (like stripes or polka dots), then bring it to life with flavors from our winter pantry and fun holiday treats. Arrange it all on a round board, and top the board off with a ribbon to complete the festive look.

Shopping List

CHEESE

Cranberry chèvre (page 49, or store-bought)

Grand Cru, Manchego, or Gouda

Havarti

MEAT

Hard salami

PRODUCE

Pomegranate arils

Other red produce, such as cherries, raspberries, or red grapes (optional)

Sugared Cranberries (optional; page 37)

CRUNCH

Festive crackers (such as Valley LahVosh's Tree Crackers)

Holiday cookies

Marcona almonds

Shelled pistachios

ACCOUTREMENTS

Cornichons

Spiced cherry jam

BUILD IT

Prep: Prepare the Cranberry Chèvre (if desired; page 49). Wash and dry all produce. Slice the Grand Cru into thin triangular slices. Slice the cranberry chèvre into ¼-inch (.5cm) slices. Cut the havarti into square or rectangular shapes, or use small holiday cookie cutters to cut out shapes. Thinly slice the salami. Add the marcona almonds, jam, and cornichons to small bowls.

Build: Place the bowls of **marcona almonds (1), jam (2),** and **cornichons (3)** in a row across the middle of the board. Arrange the **Grand Cru (4), Cranberry Chèvre (5),** and **havarti (6)** in three rows across the board. Continue adding rows with the **salami (7), pomegranate arils** and **other red produce (8), crackers (9), cookies (10),** and **pistachios (11).** Garnish with **Sugared Cranberries (12)** (if using).

Serve: Enjoy immediately or cover and refrigerate until 20 to 30 minutes before serving.

Deck the halls!
A festive
ornament-shaped
cheese board
adds a whimsical
twist to your
holiday table.

CRANBERRY CHÈVRE

Cranberry chèvre is typically available at most grocery stores in the fall and winter months, but if you can't find it or prefer homemade, here's a simple recipe to make it yourself.

MAKES: 1 (8 oz/225g) log
TOTAL TIME: 15 minutes

8 oz (225g) log chèvre	½ tsp ground
1 cup dried cranberries	cinnamon (optional)

1. Lay a sheet of parchment paper on your work surface. Carefully remove the chèvre log from its packaging and set aside for 10 minutes to come to room temperature.

2. Meanwhile, roughly chop the dried cranberries. If using cinnamon, add to a small bowl, along with the cranberries, and mix.

3. Pour the chopped cranberries onto the parchment paper, creating a thin layer slightly longer and wider than the log of chèvre.

4. Gently roll the chèvre in the cranberries. Repeat as needed until the log is coated. Use your fingers to press the dried cranberries into any open spaces.

POP, FIZZ, CHEESE BOARD

Take it from me: there is no better way to ring in a new year than with a glass of Champagne in one hand and cheese in the other! This board is filled with perfect pairings to enjoy with your favorite glass of bubbles, whether you prefer to sip them at a sparkly soiree with friends and family or on the sofa for a cozy, quiet evening watching the ball drop.

Shopping List

CHEESE
Gorgonzola Dolce or other blue cheese
Parmigiano-Reggiano
Triple-crème cheese (such as Saint-André)

MEAT
Prosciutto
Truffle salami

PRODUCE
Sugared Green Grapes (prepare using Sugared Cranberries & Rosemary recipe; page 37)
Pears
Pomegranate arils
Raspberries
Sage

CRUNCH
Breadsticks
Candied pecans
Fig and olive crisps
Taralli crackers
Truffle marcona almonds

ACCOUTREMENTS
Dark chocolate
Dried citrus
Honey
Honeycomb
Raspberry jam

EXTRAS
Leftover Christmas cookies and candy (optional)

BUILD IT

Prep: Make the Sugared Green Grapes (page 37; see the note). Wash and dry all produce. Use the tip of a knife to break off bite-sized pieces of Parmigiano-Reggiano. Thinly slice the truffle salami. Thinly slice the pears. Add the jam and honey to small bowls.

Build: Arrange the **Parmigiano-Reggiano (1)**, **triple-crème cheese (2)**, and **Gorgonzola Dolce (3)** near the edges of the board. Place the bowls of **jam (4)** and **honey (5)**. Place 2 to 3 bunches of **Sugared Green Grapes (6)**, piles of **raspberries (7)**, and stacks of **pears (8)**.

Fold the **prosciutto (9)**, and tuck it into an open space. Build a neat pile or fanned arrangement with the **truffle salami (10)**. Create stacked arrangements of **crackers (11), crisps (12), breadsticks (13)**, and **cookies and candy (14)** (if using). Add the **chocolate (15)** to open spaces. Fill in the gaps with **pomegranate arils (16), marcona almonds (17)**, and **pecans (18)**. Top the Gorgonzola Dolce with **honeycomb (19)**, and garnish the rest of the board with **dried citrus (20)** and **sage (21)**.

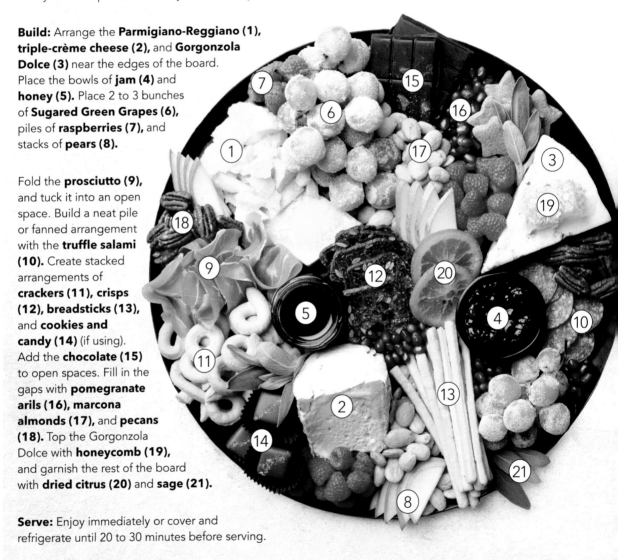

Serve: Enjoy immediately or cover and refrigerate until 20 to 30 minutes before serving.

Note: For an added New Year's Eve twist, substitute Prosecco or Champagne for the water in your simple syrup and let the grapes soak for an extra 15 to 30 minutes.

SPARKLING WINE & CHEESE PAIRINGS

Like all wine and cheese pairings, pairing cheese with sparkling wine is all about striking the right balance of flavor and texture (or mouthfeel). When that balance is achieved, each element is enhanced and transformed, resulting in a truly special tasting experience.

While I always say that there are no strict rules when it comes to pairings (it's all about what you love), there are a few helpful tips to keep in mind when selecting cheeses to pair with Champagne and other sparkling wines:

- The wine should be more acidic than the cheese. Goat cheese, for example, has a higher level of acidity than Brie (think about the light tang of creamy chèvre) and is therefore a great match with Cava, which is less acidic than Champagne.

- By the same principle, the wine should be sweeter than the cheese. Sweet sparkling wines like Asti Spumante and Moscato become overpowered by cheeses with sweeter notes like English cheddar or Gouda, but the funky saltiness of blue cheese is the perfect foil.

- When it comes to texture (or mouthfeel), in general, the effervescence of sparkling wines can stand up to creamy and hard cheeses alike, but the texture of the cheese can have a big impact on how the combination plays out on your palette. As you experiment with pairings, notice how the bubbles in Champagne "scrub" your palette after a bite of a buttery triple-crème cheese, and in comparison, how the bubbles take a back seat to the flavors of the wine when paired with hard Gruyère.

With these tips in mind, here is a guide to some perfect pairings:

CHAMPAGNE

Camembert

Gruyère and other Alpine-style cheeses, such as Comté or Uplands Cheese's Pleasant Ridge Reserve

Washed-rind cheeses, such as Langres and Époisses

PROSECCO

Aged Gouda

Parmigiano-Reggiano and Grana Padano

Triple-crèmes, such as Saint-André and Cowgirl Creamery's Mt. Tam

Robiola

CAVA

Brie or Camembert

Sheep's-milk cheeses, such as Ossau-Iraty and Manchego

Soft goat cheeses, such as chèvre and Caña de Cabra

ASTI SPUMANTE

Creamy blue cheeses, such as Gorgonzola Dolce, Jasper Hill Farm's Bayley Hazen Blue, and Point Reyes Bay Blue

NEW YEAR'S EVE DESSERT BOARD

Tick! Tock! Count down to the new year with a whimsical dessert board filled with sweet and salty treats. Chocolate is the name of the game, but the sky's the limit when it comes to ingredients, so get the whole family involved as you build your shopping list with everyone's favorite sweets!

Shopping List

CHEESE

Aged cheddar (such as Milton Creamery's Prairie Breeze and Barber's 1833 Cheddar—both have a hint of sweetness that complement the flavors on this board)

Brie

Espresso BellaVitano

PRODUCE

Black & White Chocolate–Dipped Clementines & Strawberries (page 57)

Raspberries

CRUNCH

Chocolate-covered pretzels

Cookies (such as Biscoff, Pirouette, shortbread, and stroopwafels)

ACCOUTREMENTS

Chocolate-covered caramels

Chocolate-covered espresso beans

Ferrero Rocher Truffles

Marshmallows

Peanut butter cups

Other sweet treats (optional)

BUILD IT

For little hands: While you build the board, have the kids make the clock hands with cardstock and a brad paper fastener (optional).

Prep: Wash and dry the berries. Make Black & White Chocolate–Dipped Clementines & Strawberries (page 57). Slice the cheddar into thin rectangular slices. Use the tip of a knife to break off bite-sized pieces of BellaVitano.

Build: Arrange the **aged cheddar (1)**, **BellaVitano (2)**, and **Brie (3)** near the edges of the board. Create neat piles or fanned arrangements of the **chocolate-covered pretzels (4)** and **cookies (5)**. Build piles of **raspberries (6)** and the **Black & White Chocolate-Dipped Clementines & Strawberries (7)**. Fill in the open spaces with piles of the remaining accoutrements: **chocolate-covered espresso beans (8), chocolate-covered caramels (9), Ferrero Rocher Truffles (10), peanut butter cups (11),** and **marshmallows (12).**

Serve: Add the clock hands for the finishing touch (optional), and enjoy immediately.

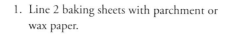

BLACK & WHITE CHOCOLATE-DIPPED CLEMENTINES & STRAWBERRIES

The classic flavors of chocolate-dipped strawberries and citrus get a New Year's Eve twist with a mix of dark chocolate and white chocolate coating.

MAKES: 1 lb (450g) strawberries and 6–8 clementines

TOTAL TIME: 45 minutes

---

1 lb (450g) strawberries

14 oz (400g) dark chocolate melting discs

14 oz (400g) white chocolate melting discs

Flaky sea salt

6–8 clementines

---

1. Line 2 baking sheets with parchment or wax paper.

2. Wash the strawberries and allow to dry completely.

3. Peel the clementines and gently remove all skin and pith. Separate into individual segments and arrange in a single layer on a paper towel to dry.

4. Prepare the chocolate melting discs according to package instructions.

5. When the fruit is dry and the chocolates are melted, dip the fruit as follows:

CLEMENTINES

1. Holding a clementine segment gently by the top, dip halfway into the dark chocolate at a slight angle, covering half of the segment. Lift straight out of the chocolate and allow excess to drip back into the bowl or pot. Lay flat onto the lined baking sheet to dry.

2. Repeat until half of the clementines have been dipped with the dark chocolate. As you work and the chocolate cools on the clementines you've dipped, sprinkle a small pinch of flaky sea salt onto the semidry chocolate.

3. Repeat steps 1 and 2 with the white chocolate and the remaining clementines.

4. Allow to dry completely. Refrigerate in an airtight container.

STRAWBERRIES

1. Holding a strawberry by the stem, dip into the dark chocolate at a slight angle, covering three-fourths of the berry. Lift straight out of the chocolate and allow excess to drip back into the bowl or pot. Lay flat onto the lined baking sheet to dry.

2. Repeat until all of the strawberries have been dipped with the dark chocolate at an angle.

3. When the chocolate has dried, repeat steps 1 and 2 with the white chocolate, dipping on the opposite side of the strawberry to create an overlapping criss-cross effect. For best results, follow up with a second coat of the white chocolate.

4. Repeat with all strawberries and allow to dry completely. Refrigerate in an airtight container.

SNOW DAY FONDUE BOARD

One of the first times I remember eating fondue was in elementary school at a fondue party organized by a friend's mom. There were stations set up around the kitchen with a variety of fondues and a seemingly endless array of items for dipping—it was truly a dream! But the best part was the cozy feeling of gathering with friends around the warm fondue pots, filling our skewers with delicious bites and trying new combinations together. This fondue board is inspired by that cozy feeling and is one of my favorite ways to gather for a meal on a cold, snowy day.

Shopping List

CHEESE
Swiss Fondue (page 61, or store-bought)

MEAT
Assorted meats for dipping, such as hard salami, ham, roasted chicken, beef, or kielbasa

CRUNCH
Crusty bread
Mixed nuts
Pretzels

PRODUCE
Asparagus
Broccolini
Carrots
Green apples
Radishes
Red grapes
Rosemary
Microgreens (optional)

ACCOUTREMENTS
Cornichons

SUPPLIES
Skewers

BUILD IT

Prep: Wash and dry all produce, and trim or slice as desired. Slice the meats and bread into bite-sized pieces. Make the Swiss Fondue (if desired; page 61).

Build: Keeping a space open for the fondue pot, begin adding sections of the **assorted meats (1).**

Create neat piles of the veggies: **radishes (2), carrots (3), asparagus (4),** and **broccolini (5).** Add the **bread (6)** and **pretzels (7).** Add 2 to 3 bunches of **grapes (8)** and stacks of **apple slices (9).** Fill in any gaps with **mixed nuts (10)** and **cornichons (11).** Garnish with **rosemary (12)** and **microgreens (13)** (if using).

Place the pot of **Swiss Fondue (14).**

Serve: Serve with individual skewers for dipping and enjoy immediately.

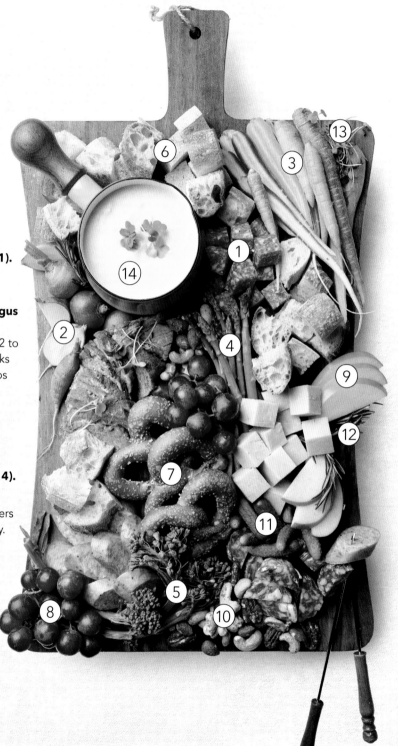

The distinct, nutty flavor of classic Swiss fondue complements an assortment of savory bites.

SWISS FONDUE

A classic combination of two Alpine cheeses and traditional ingredients yields a silky fondue with a distinct nutty flavor.

MAKES: 6–8 servings

TOTAL TIME: 25 minutes

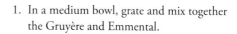

¾ lb (340g) Gruyère

¾ lb (340g) Emmental or other Swiss cheese

1 clove garlic, halved

1 cup dry white wine

1½ tbsp cornstarch

1½ tbsp kirsch liqueur (optional)

Kosher salt and freshly ground black pepper, to taste

Pinch of freshly grated nutmeg (optional)

1. In a medium bowl, grate and mix together the Gruyère and Emmental.

2. Season the fondue pot (see the note) by rubbing the bottom and sides with the cut garlic clove. Discard the garlic. (Or, if you prefer a stronger garlic flavor, keep the garlic in the pot.)

3. Place over medium heat, and add the wine and cornstarch. Stir to combine. Heat the mixture, stirring occasionally, until smooth and thickened slightly.

4. Add one handful of cheese and whisk, letting it melt and combine with the wine completely before adding the next handful. Repeat until you have a smooth, silky sauce.

5. Once all of the cheese has been added and is completely melted, stir in the kirsch (if using). Season with salt, pepper, and nutmeg (if using) to taste. Serve immediately.

Note: If you don't have a stove-safe fondue pot or are serving your fondue in a smaller dish, you can prepare the fondue in any stove-safe pot.

ALL ABOUT
CHARCUTERIE BOARD

Let's talk about charcuterie. We eat it; we talk about it; we Instagram it—but what is it, *really*? *Charcuterie* (pronounced *shar-koo-tuh-ree*) is French for "delicatessen" and is also the term for the art of preparing meats like bacon, ham, sausage—as well as charcuterie board favorites like prosciutto and salami. While cheese is often the star of a board, this board's variety of meats lets charcuterie step into the spotlight.

Shopping List

CHEESE

(1) Brie, Camembert, or other bloomy rind cheese
(2) Gruyère
(3) P'tit Basque

MEAT

(4) Bresaola
(5) Capicola
(6) Hard salami
(7) Prosciutto
(8) Sopressata

PRODUCE

(9) Blackberries
(10) Pears
(11) Red grapes
(12) Rosemary
(12) Sage

CRUNCH

(13) Flatbread crackers
(14) Fruit and nut crisps
Baguette or breadsticks (optional)

ACCOUTREMENTS

(15) Cornichons
(16) Dried fruit (such as cranberries, cherries, or apricots)
(17) Fig jam
(18) Grainy mustard
(19) Honey
(20) Olives

Prep: Wash, dry, and prep all produce. Cut the Gruyère and salami into thin slices. Add the jam, honey, and mustard to small bowls. **Build:** Arrange the ingredients on the board. **Serve:** Enjoy immediately or cover and refrigerate until 20 to 30 minutes before serving.

WINTER BRUNCH BOARD

When the hustle and bustle of the holiday season has died down and the doldrums of winter have settled in, hosting a winter brunch is just what the doctor ordered! For an elevated twist on your brunch menu, create a beautiful cheese board with light, creamy cheeses to pair with beautiful fresh pastries and seasonal fruit.

Shopping List

CHEESE

(1) Cranberry or honey chèvre

(2) Fromager d'Affinois (or other creamy, bloomy rind cheese)

MEAT

(3) Prosciutto

CRUNCH

(4) Fresh pastries (such as croissants, danishes, etc.)

PRODUCE

(5) Citrus (such as oranges or grapefruit)

(6) Raspberries

(7) Rosemary

(7) Sage

(8) Strawberries

ACCOUTREMENTS

(9) Crème fraîche

(10) Honey

(11) Raspberry jam

Prep: Wash, dry, and prep all produce. Slice the chèvre into rounds. Add the crème fraîche, jam, and honey to small bowls. **Build:** Arrange the ingredients on the board. **Serve:** Enjoy immediately with your favorite brunch beverages.

VALENTINE'S DAY SWEETHEART BOARD

Just you, me, and a wheel of Brie. Whether your ideal Valentine's Day date involves a big romantic night out or a cozy night at home, make it extra sweet with a romantic board filled with delicious cheeses, accoutrements, and special Valentine's Day treats.

Shopping List

CHEESE

(1) Goat milk Gouda (such as Cypress Grove's Midnight Moon)

(2) Brie

(3) Vintage cheddar

MEAT

(4) Prosciutto

(5) Sopressata

PRODUCE

(6) Cherries

(7) Raspberries

(8) Sage

(9) Strawberries

CRUNCH

(10) Fig and olive crisps

(11) Macarons or other cookies, such as gingersnaps or biscotti

(12) Marcona almonds

ACCOUTREMENTS

(13) Chocolate or Valentine's Day candy

(14) Honey

(15) Strawberry jam

Prep: Wash, dry, and prep all produce. Slice the Gouda and cheddar into thin rectangular pieces. Add the jam and honey to small bowls. **Build:** Arrange the ingredients on the board. **Serve:** Enjoy immediately or cover and refrigerate until 20 to 30 minutes before serving.

VALENTINE'S DAY CHOCOLATE FONDUE BOARD

This sweet Valentine's Day board takes everything I love about fondue and remixes it, turning it into a chocolate lover's delight. The secret to a great chocolate fondue board? Really good chocolate and a variety of delicious sweet and salty bites for dipping.

Shopping List

PRODUCE

(1) Raspberries

(2) Strawberries

CRUNCH

(3) Salty, crunchy items, such as potato chips, breadsticks, or plain pretzels

SWEETS

(4) Angel food cake

(5) Brownie bites

(6) Chocolate-covered espresso beans, cherries, raisins, nuts, etc.

(7) Chocolate-covered pretzels

(8) Chocolate melting discs

(9) Chocolate morsels or sprinkles

(10) Marshmallows

(11) Oreos

(12) Stroopwafels or other cookies

SUPPLIES

Skewers

Prep: Wash, dry, and prep all produce. Cut the angel food cake into bite-sized pieces. Melt the chocolate melting discs, and add to small bowls. **Build:** Arrange the ingredients on the board. **Serve:** Serve with individual skewers for dipping, and enjoy immediately.

Spring

Your Spring Pantry

There is so much to love about spring: the days start to get longer; the air gets warmer with each passing day; flowers bloom as the earth turns green again; and fresh, vibrant produce returns to the shelves. Spring is also an exciting time to discover new cheeses as cows, goats, and sheep return to pastures filled with fresh grasses, marking the beginning of fresh cheese season (think fresh goat cheese and ricotta) and cheeses that were made the previous year reach nutty, aged perfection.

The colors and flavors of spring create endless opportunities for vibrant, delicious boards that add a special touch to any springtime occasion—from holidays to picnics and everything in between. Let's take a look at the highlights of your spring pantry:

THE PRODUCE
Apricots
Asparagus
Blackberries
Blueberries
Broccolini
Carrots
Clementines
Edible flowers
Fresh herbs
Golden berries
Grapefruits
Grapes
Kumquats
Lemons
Persian cucumbers
Raspberries
Strawberries

THE CHEESES
Alp Blossom
Brie (both cow and
 goat milk)
Camembert
Cheddar
Chèvre
Comté
Cottonbell
Elderflower cheddar
Goat milk Gouda
Gruyère
Humboldt Fog
Julianna
Kunik
Ossau-Iraty/Esquirrou
Pleasant Ridge
 Reserve
Ricotta
Robiola

THE ACCOUTREMENTS
Apricot jam
Blackberry jam
Castelvetrano olives
Cornichons
Dried apricots
Fruit and nut crisps
Gingersnaps
Herby crackers
Honey
Honeycomb
Lemon curd
Marcona almonds
Pistachios
Raspberry jam
Strawberry jam

SPRING PAIRINGS BOARD

When I think of spring, I imagine flavors and colors that are fresh and aromatic, light as a cloud and as bright—yet soft—as the daisies and lilacs blooming outside. This board brings that springtime vision to life with an array of some of the best flavors spring has to offer.

Shopping List

CHEESE
Capriole's Julianna (or another cheese that features edible flowers, such as Alp Blossom)

Herb chèvre

Ossau-Iraty

Brie (or other bloomy rind cheese, such as Boxcarr Cheese's Cottonbell or Nettle Meadow Farm's Kunik)

MEAT
Prosciutto

Salami

PRODUCE
Blackberries

Blueberries

Raspberries

Rosemary

Strawberries

Thyme

CRUNCH
Flatbread crackers

Mixed nuts

Pistachios

Rosemary-raisin crisps

ACCOUTREMENTS
Cornichons

Green olives

Honey

Raspberry jam

BUILD IT

Prep: Wash and dry all produce. Slice the strawberries in half. Slice the Ossau-Iraty into thin, triangular slices. Cut a few slices of Julianna, leaving the rest whole to show off the beautiful dried flowers. Slice the chèvre into rounds. Add the jam, honey, and cornichons to small bowls.

Build: Arrange the **Ossau-Iraty (1), Julianna (2), herb chèvre (3),** and **Brie (4)** near the edges of the board. Place the bowls of **jam (5), honey (6),** and **cornichons (7).** Create a few piles each of **strawberries (8), raspberries (8),** and **blackberries (9),** adding a few **blueberries (9)** to the blackberry piles for visual interest.

Fold the **prosciutto (10)** and **salami (11),** and add them to open spaces. Create layered arrangements of **crackers (12)** and **crisps (13).** Fill in the gaps with piles of **olives (14), pistachios (15),** and **mixed nuts (16).** Garnish with **rosemary** and **thyme (17)** and a couple of strawberries on top of the Brie.

Serve: Enjoy immediately or cover and refrigerate until 20 to 30 minutes before serving.

Enjoy this celebration of spring flavors to mix and match as you explore pairings and discover your new favorite bite.

| PAIRINGS | The creamy textures and mild complexities of these cheeses make them perfectly suited for pairing with seasonal ingredients. Try these combinations for balanced bites that enhance and transform each flavor. |

HERB CHÈVRE

Blackberries
Flatbread crackers
Salami

JULIANNA

Flatbread crackers
Honey
Pistachios
Prosciutto
Raspberries

OSSAU-IRATY

Mixed nuts
Olives
Raspberry jam
Rosemary-raisin crisps
Salami

BRIE

Honey
Prosciutto
Raspberries
Rosemary-raisin crisps
Strawberries

SWEET AS HONEY BOARD

Honey is a classic cheese board accoutrement, and for good reason! The complex, sweet flavor profile and beautiful, golden hue of honey enhances and transforms the flavor, color, and texture of creamy cheese and salty charcuterie, making it the simplest way to elevate any board. For a buzzworthy tasting experience, gather around this beautiful board filled with spring flavors to pair with a variety of honeys.

Shopping List

CHEESE

BellaVitano Gold

Comté

Roquefort (or substitute with a light and fresh cheese such as chèvre or ricotta, if preferred)

Triple-crème cheese (such as Saint-André)

MEAT

Prosciutto

PRODUCE

Apricots

Cherries

Raspberries

Sage

Strawberries

CRUNCH

Effie's Oatcakes (or any slightly sweet tea biscuit)

Flatbread crackers

Gingersnaps

Pistachios

ACCOUTREMENTS

Honey (2–3 varieties)

Honeycomb (optional)

BUILD IT

Prep: Wash and dry all produce. Slice the strawberries and apricots in half. Slice the Comté into thin rectangular pieces. Use the tip of a knife to break off bite-sized pieces of BellaVitano. Add the honeys to small bowls.

Build: Arrange the bowls of **honey (1)** vertically down the center of the board and place the **Comté (2), triple-crème cheese (3), BellaVitano (4),** and **Roquefort (5)** near the edges of the board.

Add a few piles of **strawberries** and **raspberries (6).** Arrange sections of **apricots (7)** and small bunches of **cherries (8).** Fold the **prosciutto (9),** and add it two small sections. Create stacked and fanned arrangements of **crackers (10), Oatcakes (11),** and **cookies (12).** Fill in the gaps with **pistachios (13),** and garnish with **sage (14).** Add a small piece of honeycomb (if using) on top of the triple-crème cheese.

Serve: Enjoy immediately or cover and refrigerate until 20 to 30 minutes before serving. Serve with honey dippers or spoons for the honey.

HONEY PAIRINGS

- Invest in quality local honeys for their complex, distinct flavors. As you taste your honeys, pay attention to how the flavors range from floral to marshmallowy sweet.

- For balance, pair honeys and cheeses with equal intensity (e.g., a delicate, floral honey with Brie).

- For contrast, pair honeys and cheeses with opposite intensity (e.g., a light, sweet honey with blue cheese).

- Add a few varieties of honey to allow guests to mix and match and discover what they love. Tip: A honey dipper is the perfect way to drizzle!

- In addition to flavor variety, incorporate different textures—thin, whipped, creamy, or even honeycomb!

Sweet honey and salty cheese create a perfectly balanced bite.

LUCK OF THE IRISH BOARD

As the saying goes: Everyone's Irish on St. Patrick's Day! From traditional Irish foods to joyful celebrations filled with rainbows and leprechauns, it's a holiday the whole family can enjoy. While there's no pot of gold at the end of this rainbow, a variety of colorful fruit, mozzarella "clouds," and whimsical details would have even the grumpiest leprechaun agreeing that this board is magically delicious.

Shopping List

CHEESE

Mini or bite-sized fresh mozzarella (often called ciliegine)

White cheddar or havarti

PRODUCE

Blackberries

Blueberries

Clementines

Golden berries

Green apples

Green grapes

Oranges

Raspberries

Red grapes

Strawberries

ACCOUTREMENTS

Chocolate coins

SUPPLIES

Shamrock cookie cutter

BUILD IT

Prep: Wash and dry all produce. Cut the strawberries in half. Thinly slice the green apples. Peel and segment the clementines. Cut the oranges into slices. Use a cookie cutter to cut out shamrock shapes with the havarti. Add the mozzarella to two small bowls.

Build: Using **strawberries, red grapes,** and **raspberries (1),** arrange the top arch of the rainbow design diagonally across the board. Finish the rainbow design with a row of **clementines, oranges,** and **golden berries (2);** a row of **green grapes** and **green apples (3);** a row of **blackberries** and **blueberries (4);** and a final row of **chocolate coins (5).** Add the bowls of **mozzarella (6)** to each end of the rainbow design to mimic clouds. Garnish with the **havarti (7)** shamrock cutouts.

Serve: Enjoy immediately or cover and refrigerate until 20 to 30 minutes before serving.

STYLING TIP: COLOR

You've likely noticed how colorful the boards in this book are—and that's not an accident! Aside from choosing quality ingredients, color is the most important factor when creating a cheese board. Why? Well, as the saying goes: We eat with our eyes first.

Cheese and charcuterie are beautiful ingredients in their own right, but their neutral, one-dimensional colors tend to fall flat when presented alone on a board. It takes the addition of colorful produce and accoutrements to bring those ingredients to life and create something that is as exciting to look at as it is to eat.

So what's the best way to incorporate color? I like to approach it by creating a cohesive color story with the fruit, jam, nuts, garnishes, and even the tones of the cheeses I choose.

A color story can be inspired by the season, a location, a holiday, a party theme, or a bouquet of flowers. Choose the color story you want to create before heading to the store, and keep it in mind as you choose your ingredients.

Choosing the color story and ingredients is just the beginning. As you learned on page 20, the key to an elevated, show-stopping board is in the styling. As you build your board, think through the placement of each item, adding pockets of color throughout to create variety and visual interest that draws the eye around the board, allowing your guests to take in every delicious ingredient.

The most important thing to remember when it comes to color is that it's all about creating something joyful and fun! There are no hard and fast rules, so get creative and let your imagination be your guide.

SPRING CRUDITÉS BOARD

Sometimes the occasion calls for veggies and dip. When that moment comes, skip the premade tray at the grocery store, and instead fill your shopping basket with a variety of the season's best produce. This board is a show-stopper, but trust me: with the styling tricks you've learned along the way (color, texture, variety), you'll be amazed at how quickly it comes together.

Shopping List

PRODUCE

Asparagus

Broccolini

Cherry tomatoes

Dill

Multicolored carrots

Persian cucumbers

Purple cauliflower

Radishes

Snap peas

ACCOUTREMENTS

Hummus

Crackers or pita
(for serving)

BUILD IT

Prep: Prep the vegetables and hummus according to the styling tips on page 89.

Build: Place the bowl of **hummus (1)** in the center or just off-center on the board or platter. Add sections of **broccolini (2), carrots (3), cucumbers (4), purple cauliflower (5), snap peas (6), cherry tomatoes (7), asparagus (8),** and **radishes (9)** around the perimeter of the board. Continue layering and adding veggies in any open spaces to add visual interest and texture. Garnish with **dill (10).**

Serve: Enjoy immediately or cover and refrigerate until ready to serve. Serve with crackers or pita on the side.

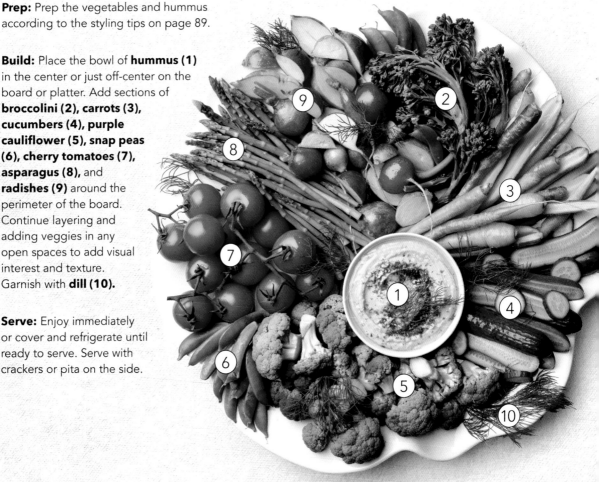

Crudités (pronounced "kroo-dee-tay") is an appetizer of assorted raw vegetables, usually served with a dip or sauce.

STYLING TIPS: VEGETABLES & HUMMUS

Prepping Vegetables:

- Wash all of the vegetables with a produce wash or make your own with a mix of 1 part vinegar and 4 parts water.
- Trim the stems and leaves from the carrots, broccolini, and radishes. Break off the woody ends from the asparagus.
- When it comes to cutting vegetables, remember that a variety of shapes and sizes will add visual interest to your presentation. For example, you could slice most of the carrots and radishes in half lengthwise, but leave some whole. You could slice one cucumber into thin coins, but cut the remaining in half or into spears.
- For more tender broccolini and asparagus, blanch them in salted boiling water for 2 to 4 minutes. Remove from the boiling water and let dry. Blanching will also result in a brighter green color.

Styling Hummus:

- Neatly transfer the hummus from its packaging into a small serving bowl. Or for a no-mess option, keep it in its original container.
- Using the back of a spoon, create a swirl across the top of the hummus.
- Lightly drizzle ½ tablespoon of extra-virgin olive oil over the hummus.
- Garnish with fresh dill, flaky sea salt, and seasonings like za'atar or everything bagel seasoning.

CHÈVRE FORÈVRE BOARD

Fresh goat cheese (or chèvre) is the hallmark of spring in the cheese world. The goat milk collected at the very beginning of the season results in the cloud-like creamy texture and light flavor with just a hint of tang. I love fresh goat cheese for its versatility: use it to top salads, spread it on toast with a drizzle of honey, or serve it alongside sweet and savory accompaniments for a delicious springtime appetizer.

Shopping List

CHEESE

Herb Chèvre (page 93, or store-bought)

Marinated Chèvre (page 93, or store-bought)

Whipped Honey Chèvre (page 93, or store-bought)

MEAT

Capicola

Prosciutto

PRODUCE

Blackberries

Blueberries

Rosemary

Strawberries

Thyme

CRUNCH

Baguette

Flatbread crackers

Mixed nuts

ACCOUTREMENTS

Cornichons

Green olives

Honeycomb

Strawberry jam

BUILD IT

Prep: Prepare the three chèvres according to the recipes on page 93. Wash and dry all produce. Slice the strawberries in half. Toast the baguette slices, if desired. Slice a few rounds of the Herb Chèvre. Add the Marinated Chèvre, Whipped Honey Chèvre, and jam to small bowls.

Build: Arrange the **Herb Chèvre (1), Marinated Chèvre (2),** and **Whipped Chèvre (3)** around the perimeter of the board. Place the bowl of **jam (4).**

Build small piles of **strawberries (5)** and **blackberries (6),** adding a few **blueberries (6)** to the blackberry piles. Add at least two sections of each of these elements for variety and visual interest.

Fold the **prosciutto (7)** and **capicola (8),** and arrange them in open spaces. Create fanned arrangements of **crackers (9)** and **baguette (10).** Add a piece of **honeycomb (11)** and piles of **olives (12), cornichons (13),** and **mixed nuts (14)** to remaining open spaces. Garnish with **rosemary** and **thyme (15).**

Serve: Enjoy immediately.

Chèvre (pronounced shev-ruh) is French for "goat" and refers to bright and tangy fresh goat cheese.

MARINATED CHÈVRE

MAKES: 8 oz (225g)
TOTAL TIME: 15 minutes, plus at least 1 hour to marinate

---

8 oz (225g) log plain chèvre

Fresh thyme

Fresh oregano

Fresh rosemary

½ tsp whole peppercorns

Pinch of red pepper flakes

½ tsp lemon zest

Kosher salt

Extra-virgin olive oil

---

1. Using a sharp knife or unflavored dental floss, slice the chèvre into 1-inch (2.5cm) cubes. Place the cubes in a jar, leaving a bit of headspace.

2. Add the thyme, oregano, and rosemary sprigs to taste, or about 6 sprigs of each. Add the peppercorns, red pepper flakes, lemon zest, and a pinch of kosher salt.

3. Pour extra-virgin olive oil into the jar to completely cover the cheese.

4. Seal the jar. Marinate for 1 to 2 hours at room temperature, or up to 1 week in the refrigerator. Bring to room temperature 1 to 2 hours before serving.

HERB CHÈVRE

MAKES: 4 oz (110g) log
TOTAL TIME: 15 minutes

---

2 tbsp finely chopped fresh parsley

2 tbsp finely chopped fresh chives

½ tsp lemon zest

4 oz (110g) log plain chèvre

---

1. Lay a sheet of parchment paper on your work surface.

2. In a small bowl, mix together the parsley and chives. Mix in the lemon zest to combine.

3. Pour the herb mixture onto the parchment paper, spreading it into a thin layer slightly longer and wider than the chèvre log.

4. Remove the chèvre from its packaging and place on the parchment paper at one end of the herb mixture.

5. Gently roll the goat cheese in the mixed herbs. Repeat as needed until the surface is coated.

WHIPPED HONEY CHÈVRE

MAKES: 1 cup
TOTAL TIME: 10 minutes

---

8 oz (225g) log plain chèvre

¼ cup whipped cream cheese

1 tbsp honey, plus extra for garnish

½ tsp lemon zest, plus extra for garnish

Pinch of kosher salt

Fresh thyme (optional)

---

1. Bring the chèvre and cream cheese to room temperature.

2. To a food processor or medium bowl, add the chèvre, cream cheese, honey, lemon zest, and salt. Beat until combined and a creamy, fluffy consistency.

3. Add the whipped chèvre to a clean bowl or ramekin. Garnish with a drizzle of honey and a sprinkle of lemon zest and fresh thyme (if using).

MOTHER'S DAY BOARD

Mother's Day is all about celebrating the most important women in our lives: our mothers, grandmothers, aunts, and mother figures of all kinds. Inspired by my own mom and the cherished memories we've made while creating beautiful, delicious meals together, this board is the perfect way to celebrate.

Surprise Mom with the beautiful arrangement or have her join in on the fun as you arrange the variety of extra-special cheeses and sweet, springy accents like macarons and salami roses. (Learn how to make them on page 97.)

Shopping List

CHEESE
Chardonnay BellaVitano
Fromager d'Affinois (or
  triple-crème cheese)
Humboldt Fog

MEAT
Prosciutto
Salami

PRODUCE
Raspberries
Red grapes
Rosemary
Sage
Strawberries

CRUNCH
Fig and olive crisps
Flatbread crackers
Macarons
Marcona almonds

ACCOUTREMENTS
Castelvetrano olives
Honey
Raspberry jam

BUILD IT

Prep: Wash and dry all produce. Slice the strawberries in half. Add the jam and honey to small bowls. Create two salami roses in small bowls (page 97). Add the honey and jam to small bowls. Use the tip of a knife to break off bite-sized pieces of BellaVitano.

Build: Arrange the **Humboldt Fog (1)**, **Fromager d'Affinois (2),** and **BellaVitano (3)** near the edges of the board. Place the bowls of **jam (4), honey (5),** and **salami roses (6).** Add bunches of **grapes (7)** and piles of **strawberries** and **raspberries (8),** and **olives (9).**

Fold and place the **prosciutto (10).** Create stacked arrangements of **crackers (11), crisps (12),** and **macarons (13).** Fill in the gaps with **marcona almonds (14).** Garnish with **sage** and **rosemary (15).** Add a few raspberries and sage leaves on top of the Fromager d'Affinois.

Serve: Enjoy immediately or cover and refrigerate until 20 to 30 minutes before serving.

Add a touch of spring to your boards by transforming salami into beautiful, edible roses.

Step 1: Arrange about 10 slices of salami in a long row with the edges overlapping.

Step 2: Carefully fold the row of layered salami in half.

Step 3: Starting on either end of the folded row, carefully roll up the salami. **Tip:** Create a very tight spiral with the first piece because it will become the center of the "rose."

Step 4: Place the salami rose in a ramekin or small bowl with the folded edge facing down. Use your fingers to carefully loosen some of the "petals" to give it a more natural look.

BERRY BASKET BOARD

One of the things I look forward to most each spring is the return of sweet, juicy berries. Berries are a natural accompaniment to cheese because their bright, sweet flavors complement light, creamy cheeses and salty, aged cheeses alike. This board is overflowing with berries, offering a variety of delicious pairing possibilities.

Shopping List

CHEESE

(1) Brie
(2) White cheddar
(3) Whole-milk
ricotta (1 cup)

MEAT

(4) Prosciutto
(5) Sopressata

PRODUCE

(6) Blackberries
(6) Blueberries
(7) Mint
(8) Raspberries
(9) Rosemary
(10) Strawberries

CRUNCH

(11) Almonds
(12) Angel food cake
(13) Baguette
(14) Taralli crackers

ACCOUTREMENTS

(15) Honey

Raspberry or
strawberry jam
(optional)

Prep: Wash, dry, and prep all produce. Thinly slice the baguette. Cut the angel food cake into bite-sized cubes. In a medium bowl, whip 2 tablespoons honey, a pinch of salt, and the ricotta until fluffy; add to a small bowl. Cut the cheddar into thin rectangular pieces. Add the honey and jam (if using) to small bowls.
Build: Arrange the ingredients on the board.
Serve: Enjoy immediately.

SPRING COLORS BOARD

Soft and light meets bright and vibrant. This combination of ingredients from your spring pantry creates a fresh, springy color palette that perfectly complements the flavors, textures, and even the aromas on this board. It's truly a feast for all of your senses!

CHEESE

(1) Brie
(2) Cheddar
(3) Cypress Grove's Purple Haze (or other fresh goat cheese)

MEAT

(4) Capicola
(5) Sopressata

PRODUCE

(6) Blackberries
(6) Blueberries
(7) Grapefruit
(8) Lavender
(9) Persian cucumbers
(8) Rosemary
(8) Sage
(8) Thyme

CRUNCH

(10) Fig and olive crisps
(11) Flatbread crackers
(12) Marcona almonds

ACCOUTREMENTS

(13) Blackberry jam
(14) Honey

Prep: Wash, dry, and prep all produce. Slice the Brie into wedges. Use the tip of a knife to break off bite-sized pieces of cheddar. Cut the Purple Haze in half. Add the jam and honey to small bowls. **Build:** Arrange the ingredients on the board. **Serve:** Enjoy immediately or cover and refrigerate until 20 to 30 minutes before serving.

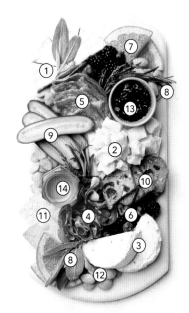

EASTER BOARD

Easter gatherings are the hallmark of spring. We search for colorful eggs and baskets of marshmallow Peeps and gather around brunch tables filled with spring flavors and vases of pastel tulips. These shared traditions are what make our holiday gatherings special, but there's always room for something new. Here's how to create a beautiful Easter board filled with spring colors and sweet accents.

Shopping List

CHEESE

(1) Brie
(2) Dill havarti
(3) Goat milk Gouda (such as Cypress Grove's Midnight Moon)

MEAT

(4) Prosciutto

PRODUCE

(5) Blueberries
(6) Raspberries
(7) Sage
(8) Strawberries

CRUNCH

(9) Flatbread crackers
(10) Gingersnaps
(11) Madeleines
(12) Pistachios
(13) Shortbread or other cookies

ACCOUTREMENTS

(14) Chocolate eggs, or other types of Easter candy
(15) Honey
(16) Lemon curd
(17) Raspberry jam

SUPPLIES

Flower cookie cutter

Prep: Wash, dry, and prep all produce. Thinly slice the goat milk Gouda and havarti. Use the flower cookie cutter to cut out the center of the brie. Fill the center with jam. Add the lemon curd, honey, and candy to small bowls.
Build: Arrange the ingredients on the board.
Serve: Enjoy immediately.

GARDEN PARTY BRUNCH BOARD

What is it about spring that just screams brunch? Perhaps it's the return of warm weather and al fresco dining, or perhaps it's our busy social calendars filled with holidays, showers, and impromptu celebrations. Whatever the reason, I can promise you one thing: serving brunch on a board makes it that much better.

Shopping List

PRODUCE

(1) Blueberries
(2) Grapefruit
(3) Oranges
(4) Raspberries
(5) Strawberries

CRUNCH

(6) Bagels
(7) Granola
(8) Pastries
 (croissants, scones, muffins, etc.)

ACCOUTREMENTS

(9) Butter
(10) Cream cheese
 (2 varieties)
(11) Honey
(12) Yogurt
(13) Edible flowers
 (optional)

Jam (optional)

Prep: Wash, dry, and prep all produce. Add the cream cheeses, honey, yogurt, and jam (if using) to small bowls. Slice the bagels in half. **Build:** Arrange the ingredients on the board. **Serve:** Enjoy immediately.

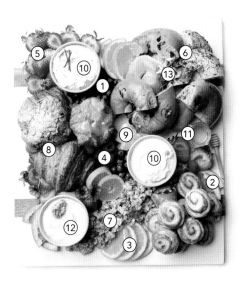

Summer

Your
Summer
Pantry

Sweet, sweet summertime. I love the way life slows down during the summer. By the time Memorial Day comes around, it's as though we've all made a collective agreement that it's time to take a breath, bask in the sunshine, embark on adventures, and savor those seemingly endless summer days with our favorite people.

The boards in this chapter are a reflection of that carefree state of mind. They are centered around simple lists of fresh, summer ingredients and are effortless to create. But despite their easy nature, each of these boards is something truly special to gather around—whether your summer adventures take you to your backyard, your best friend's patio, the family lake house, or a picnic in the park. Let's take a look inside our bountiful summer pantry:

The Produce:
Apricots
Basil
Blackberries
Blueberries
Cantaloupe
Champagne grapes
Cherries
Cherry plums
Cucumbers
Dragonfruit
Figs
Golden berries
Mangoes
Nectarines
Peaches
Plumcots
Plums
Raspberries
Strawberries
Thomcord grapes
Tomatoes
Watermelons

The Cheeses:
Brie
Burrata
Camembert
Caña de Cabra
Cheddar
Chèvre
Drunken Goat
Feta
Fresh mozzarella
Gorgonzola
Gouda
Halloumi
Havarti
Humboldt Fog
La Tur
Manchego
Parmigiano-Reggiano
Point Reyes Bay Blue
Port Salut
Ricotta
Robiola
Tomme

The Accoutrements:
Baguette
Cherry jam
Dried apricots
Dried cherries
Fig jam
Flatbread crackers
Honey
Honeycomb
Marcona almonds
Olives
Peach jam
Pickled veggies
Raspberry jam
Tomato jam

SUMMER PAIRINGS BOARD

If I had to describe summer in one word, that word would be *vibrant*. The colors, the flavors, the energy—everything seems bolder, brighter, and larger than life during the summer. This board reflects the vibrancy of the season with a bold color story and a curated selection of summer ingredients to mix and match as you create delicious, striking pairings.

Shopping List

CHEESE

Blue cheese

Brie

Goat milk Gouda (such as Cypress Grove's Midnight Moon)

Honey chèvre

MEAT

Prosciutto

Sopressata

PRODUCE

Apricots

Cantaloupe

Cherries

Cherry plums

Raspberries

Sage

Strawberries

CRUNCH

Flatbread crackers

Fruit and nut crisps

Marcona almonds

Mixed nuts

ACCOUTREMENTS

Fig jam

Green olives

Honey

Honeycomb

BUILD IT

Prep: Wash and dry all produce. Slice the strawberries in half and the apricots into quarter segments. Cut the cantaloupe into thin slices. Wrap the slices with prosciutto, if preferred. Use the tip of a knife to break off bite-sized pieces of blue cheese. Cut the Gouda into thin rectangular slices. Add the jam, honey, and green olives to small bowls.

Build: Arrange the **blue cheese (1), Brie (2), honey chèvre (3),** and **goat milk Gouda (4)** near the edges of the board. Place the bowls of **jam (5), honey (6),** and **green olives (7).** Add 2 to 3 fanned stacks of **cantaloupe (8).** Build a few piles each of **apricots (9), strawberries (10),** and **raspberries (11).**

Fold the **prosciutto (12)** and **sopressata (13),** and add them to open spaces. Create stacked and fanned arrangements of **crackers (14)** and **crisps (15).** Fill open spaces with **cherries (16), cherry plums (17), marcona almonds (18),** and **mixed nuts (19).** Garnish with **sage (20)** and a piece of **honeycomb (21)** on top of the honey chèvre.

Serve: Enjoy immediately or cover and refrigerate until 20 to 30 minutes before serving.

I've always been drawn to the flavors of summer: the sweet and savory combinations, the contrast of bold flavors and light textures, and the unexpected complexity of simple ingredients.

PAIRINGS

These flavors go together like a glass of lemonade on a hot sunny day: they're bright, bold, and refreshing. Here's a guide to creating delicious pairings with each of the cheeses on this board.

HONEY CHÈVRE

Fruit and nut crisps
Honey
Peaches
Prosciutto

BRIE

Flatbread crackers
Honey
Raspberries
Strawberries

BLUE CHEESE

Apricots
Cherries
Flatbread crackers
Honey
Sopressata

GOAT MILK GOUDA

Fig jam
Fruit and nut crisps
Olives
Raspberries

SUMMER ENTERTAINING BOARD

There are endless opportunities to gather during the summer months—picnics, barbecues, friends' nights, family reunions, pool parties, the list goes on and on. Whether you're hosting the party or contributing to the potluck, this board is your answer for an easy breezy appetizer that makes a big statement.

Shopping List

CHEESE

Chèvre

Humboldt Fog

Mini or bite-sized fresh mozzarella (often called ciliegine)

Port Salut

MEAT

Prosciutto

PRODUCE

Basil

Blackberries

Cantaloupe

Cherries

Peaches

CRUNCH

Baguette

Flatbread crackers

Marcona almonds

ACCOUTREMENTS

Balsamic glaze

Blackberry jam

Honey

BUILD IT

Prep: Wash and dry all produce. Thinly slice the peaches. Add the jam and honey to small bowls. Slice a few rounds of chèvre. Slice the baguette. Make the Prosciutto-Wrapped Melon and Melon Caprese Skewers (page 117).

Build: Arrange the **Humboldt Fog (1), chèvre (2),** and **Port Salut (3)** near the edges of the board. Place the bowls of **jam (4)** and **honey (5)**. Add 2 to 3 piles each of **Prosciutto-Wrapped Melon (6)** and **Melon Caprese Skewers (7)**. Build small piles of **blackberries (8), cherries (9),** and **peaches (10)**. Create fanned arrangements of **crackers (11)** and **baguette (12)**. Fill in the gaps with **marcona almonds (13)**. Garnish with **basil (14)**.

Serve: Enjoy immediately or cover and refrigerate until 20 to 30 minutes before serving.

MELON & PROSCIUTTO TWO WAYS

Sweet, juicy cantaloupe meets its match in savory, salty prosciutto in these two simple appetizers that take minutes to prepare but offer a big payoff in the flavor department.

PROSCIUTTO-WRAPPED MELON

½ of a large cantaloupe
6 oz (170g) thinly sliced prosciutto
Fresh mint or basil leaves (optional)

1. With a spoon, scoop out and discard the seeds of the cantaloupe half. Cut the cantaloupe into ½-inch (1.25cm) half moon segments and slice off the rind.

2. Cut each slice of prosciutto in half lengthwise.

3. Lay one piece of prosciutto on a cutting board, then gently wrap it around the middle of a slice of cantaloupe. Repeat with another piece of prosciutto, working your way upward to cover more of the cantaloupe. If desired, add a few small mint or basil leaves as you wrap!

4. Repeat with remaining slices of cantaloupe.

MELON CAPRESE SKEWERS

½ of a large cantaloupe (or include a mix of melons, such as honeydew and watermelon)
Mini or bite-sized fresh mozzarella (often called ciliegine)
6 oz (170g) thinly sliced prosciutto
Fresh basil leaves

Supplies:
Cocktail picks or toothpicks

1. With a spoon, scoop out and discard the seeds of the cantaloupe. With a melon baller, scoop small balls from the flesh of the melon.

2. Cut each slice of prosciutto in half, lengthwise.

3. One at a time, add ingredients to your skewers in the following order: melon ball, basil leaf, folded prosciutto half, and ball of mozzarella.

4. Repeat the pattern until the skewer is full. If using a variety of melon, alternate the colors as you go.

AROUND THE

PICNIC CHARCUTERIE BOX

Picture this: a perfect sunny day, a shady spot under your favorite tree, a cozy picnic blanket, a good book, and a personal charcuterie board packed up in a to-go container for easy transportation (and because no one invited ants to this picnic).

Any food storage container and a handful of your favorite bites are all you need for this darling and delicious picnic snack. Make it personal sized, like the one pictured here, or use a larger container to feed the whole picnic crew.

Shopping List

CHEESE
Cheddar
Chèvre

MEAT
Salami

PRODUCE
Raspberries
Red grapes
Rosemary
Strawberries
Thyme

CRUNCH
Fig and olive crisps
Flatbread crackers
Pistachios

ACCOUTREMENTS
Dried apricots
Fig jam

BUILD IT

Prep: Wash and dry all produce. Slice the strawberries in half. Slice the cheddar into thin rectangular pieces. Add the jam to a small dressing or condiment container. (Or use jam that is packaged in a mini jar.)

Build: In a small food storage container, arrange the **cheddar (1)** and **chèvre (2)** in opposite corners. Add the container of **jam (3).** Build 2 small piles of **strawberries (4)** and **raspberries (5).** Add 2 small bunches of **grapes (6).**

Fold the **salami (7),** and place it in an open spot. Fill in any gaps with **pistachios (8)** and **dried apricots (9).** Garnish with **rosemary** and **thyme (10).** Fill a second to-go container with crackers to serve on the side— no soggy crackers at this picnic!

Serve: Cover, transport, and enjoy.

The key to building a beautiful arrangement in such a small space? It's all about the layers. Build the foundation with cheeses and jam, and then work your way up, adding texture and color as you go.

It's picnic season . . . let's take our charcuterie to go!

AROUND THE

MEZZE PLATTER

A mezze board is my go-to on hot summer nights when I just can't bear the thought of firing up the oven. No-cook, big flavor, easy cleanup—this is summer dinner done right! Pick up ingredients from any grocery store or plan a trip to your favorite Middle Eastern market or Mediterranean restaurant for items like hummus, pita, and tabbouleh. Arrange your selections on a pretty platter and gather around for an evening of grazing and good conversation (bonus if you dine al fresco!).

Shopping List

CHEESE
Whipped Feta (page 125)

CRUNCH
Pita bread or crackers

PRODUCE
Cherry tomatoes
Figs (fresh or dried)
Lemons
Mixed fresh herbs (such as mint and parsley)
Persian cucumbers

ACCOUTREMENTS
Dolmas
Hummus
Marinated artichokes
Olives
Red peppers (such as roasted, peppadew, spicy, etc.)
Tabbouleh
Other Mediterranean mezze items (optional)

BUILD IT

Prep: Wash and dry all produce. Slice the cucumbers and figs in half, the lemon into wedges, and the pita into triangles. Make the Whipped Feta (page 125). Add the Whipped Feta and hummus to small bowls. Garnish the hummus with olive oil and flaky salt. Drain the olives, peppers, and any other items stored in oil.

Build: Add the bowls of **hummus (1)** and **Whipped Feta (2)** to the platter. Use the bowls as a foundation to place fanned arrangements of **pita (3)** and **dolmas (4).** Add sections of **cucumbers (5), tomatoes (6), artichokes (7), peppers (8), olives (9),** and **tabbouleh (10).** Garnish with **dried figs (11),** wedges of **lemon (12),** and **fresh herbs (13).**

Serve: Enjoy immediately.

Mezze (mez-ay) means "taste" or "snack." In Middle Eastern and Mediterranean cuisine, mezze is a selection of small dishes served as an appetizer or light meal.

WHIPPED FETA

Salty feta, zesty lemon, and fragrant herbs combine for a bright, creamy dip to serve with pita and fresh vegetables.

MAKES: 4–6 servings

TOTAL TIME: 10 minutes

---

8 oz (225g) block of feta, room temperature

½ cup Greek yogurt

1 garlic clove, smashed

Zest and juice of ½ lemon

1 tbsp chopped fresh oregano

1 tbsp chopped fresh basil

1 tbsp chopped fresh chives

2 tbsp extra-virgin olive oil, plus more to garnish

Kosher salt and freshly ground black pepper

Red pepper flakes

---

1. Break up the block of feta and add to a food processor along with the Greek yogurt.

2. Pulse until smooth and combined, 30 to 60 seconds.

3. Add the garlic, lemon zest and juice, oregano, basil, chives, olive oil, and a pinch each of salt, pepper, and red pepper flakes. Blend until well combined. Taste and add more salt and lemon juice as needed.

4. Scoop into a bowl and garnish with a drizzle of olive oil, a pinch of salt, and a sprig or two of fresh herbs. Serve immediately or cover and chill for 1 to 2 hours.

THAT'S MY JAM BOARD

No cheese board is fully dressed without a jar (or two) of jam. Whether sweet like fig jam or savory like hot pepper jam, this classic accoutrement adds flavor, color, texture, and, most importantly, variety. In other words, a good jam is the one-ingredient key to accomplishing all the elements that add up to a really special board.

Shopping List

CHEESE

Bloomy rind goat milk cheese (such as Laura Chenel's Creamy Brie)

Goat milk Gouda (such as Cypress Grove's Midnight Moon)

Triple-crème cheese (such as Saint-André)

MEAT

Capicola

Prosciutto

PRODUCE

Cherry plums

Figs (fresh or dried)

Grapes (mix of Champagne and Thomcord)

Plumcots

Raspberries

Rosemary

Sage

Strawberries

CRUNCH

Fig and olive crisps

Flatbread crackers

Marcona almonds

ACCOUTREMENTS

Castelvetrano olives

Fig jam

Strawberry jam (Maleah's Simple Strawberry Jam, page 129, or store-bought)

BUILD IT

Prep: Make Maleah's Simple Strawberry Jam (if desired; page 129). Wash and dry all produce. Slice the strawberries and plumcots in half. Slice the Gouda into thin triangular pieces. Spoon the jams into small bowls.

Build: Arrange the **triple-crème cheese (1), bloomy rind goat milk cheese (2),** and **goat milk Gouda (3)** near the edges of the board. Place the small bowls of **fig jam (4)** and **strawberry jam (5).** Add 2 to 3 bunches of **grapes (6)** and build a few piles each of **strawberries (7), raspberries (8), plumcots (9),** and **cherry plums (10).**

Fold the **prosciutto (11)** and **capicola (12)** and tuck into open spaces. Add a pile of **olives (13).** Create stacked arrangements of **crackers (14)** and **crisps (15).** Fill in any gaps with **marcona almonds (16).** Garnish with **figs (17)** and **sage** and **rosemary (18).**

Serve: Enjoy immediately or cover and refrigerate until 20 to 30 minutes before serving.

MALEAH'S SIMPLE STRAWBERRY JAM

A simple, small-batch recipe for the perfect strawberry jam from the owner of Madams Jams, Maleah Gluck.

MAKES:
1 (8 oz/ 225g) jar

TOTAL TIME:
30 minutes

---

1 lb (450g) fresh strawberries, hulled and chopped

1½ cups sugar

Juice of 1 large lemon

Pinch of salt

1. In a medium saucepan, mix the chopped strawberries, sugar, lemon juice, and salt. Place over medium-low heat and stir until the sugar is dissolved.

2. Increase the heat to medium-high and bring the mixture to a rolling boil.

3. Stir frequently, and use a whisk to mash the strawberries to the desired consistency. For a smoother consistency, use an immersion blender.

4. Continue boiling and stirring until the jam has thickened and bubbles form on the entire surface, 10 to 15 minutes.

5. When the jam reaches 220°F (105°C), remove from the heat and transfer to an 8-fluid-ounce (235ml) canning jar.

6. Cool and enjoy right away, or store in the refrigerator for up to 2 weeks.

7. To seal for longer storage, place the jar in a pot of water deep enough to fully cover it. Bring the water to a boil and boil the jar for 15 minutes. Cool the jar to room temperature, and use your finger to press down the middle of the lid. (It will stay down if properly sealed.) Store for up to 1 year.

A little bit of jam makes a big impact on the way you experience a bite of cheese. Experiment with new flavors and combinations until you find your perfect bite.

SUMMER COOKOUT BOARD

I have a theory that everything tastes better on a board, and this one is proof! Cookout classics like burgers and pasta salad are delicious on their own, but arrange them on a board complete with all the sides and fixings, and suddenly they look *and* taste that much better.

Shopping List

CHEESE
Blue cheese crumbles
Dill havarti
Monterey Jack
Sharp cheddar

MEAT
Bacon
Burger patties

PRODUCE
Avocado
Lettuce
Tomato
Red onion (optional)

CRUNCH
Potato chips (2 varieties,
 such as ruffled, barbecue,
 or kettle-cooked—you
 choose!)

ACCOUTREMENTS
Buns
Coleslaw
Ketchup
Mayonnaise
Mustard
Pasta salad
Pickles
Potato salad

BUILD IT

Prep: Wash and dry all produce. Slice the tomatoes, pickles, and avocados. Thinly slice the havarti, Monterey Jack, and cheddar. Add the condiments and salads to small bowls. Grill the bacon and burgers. Toast the buns.

Build: While the burgers and bacon are on the grill, arrange the bowls of **coleslaw (1), pasta salad (2), potato salad (3),** and **condiments (4).** Lay down a bed of lettuce, and arrange the **blue cheese crumbles (5), dill havarti (6), Monterey Jack (7), sharp cheddar (8), tomato (9),** and **avocado (10)** on top, plus an extra pile of **lettuce (11)** for burger topping. Add piles of **chips (12)** and **pickles (13).**

Add the cooked **burgers (14), bacon (15),** and toasted **buns (16).**

Serve: Let your guests go to town as they mix and match toppings and fill their plates with sides.

BYOB: Build Your Own Burger

MORE SUMMER COOKOUT BOARD IDEAS

Don't let the summer fun stop with cheeseburgers. All of those hallmark build-your-own meals—the ones you love to serve poolside or on the back porch—are perfectly suited to a big platter. Here are some of my favorite ideas:

BALLPARK FRANKS

Take yourself to the proverbial ball game with everyone's favorite hot dog fixings.

- Condiments (ketchup, relish, mustard, chili, etc.)
- Hot dogs and buns
- Onion rings
- Pigs in a blanket with cheese or mini corn dogs
- Popcorn

BRATS!

Any kind of sausage will do! Cut all of the sausage varieties in half, choose two to three distinct mustards, and let people mix and match.

- Cheese curds
- Condiments (sauerkraut, mustard, ketchup)
- German potato salad
- Grilled onions
- Grilled sausage varieties (beer brats, hot Italian sausage, kielbasa, etc.) and pretzel rolls
- Mixed fruit
- Pickled veggies

DELICATESSEN DELIGHTS

You don't need me to tell you what goes on this tray—there's nothing more delicious than the sandwich you build yourself. My strongest recommendation: go all out on the cheese options! The rest is up to you.

- Avocado
- Bacon
- Condiments
- Deli meat varieties
- Pickles
- Sliced cheese varieties
- Thick-cut deli bread
- Tomatoes

CAPRESE BOARD

Classic caprese with a twist. With a simple list of fresh, seasonal ingredients that boast bold, juicy flavors and a no-fuss assembly, this board is one you'll find yourself making again and again, whether as a quick and easy dinner or a stunning appetizer.

Shopping List

CHEESE
Burrata

Mini or bite-sized fresh mozzarella (often called ciliegine)

MEAT
Prosciutto

Sopressata

PRODUCE
Basil

Cherry tomatoes

Heirloom tomatoes (optional)

Raspberries

Strawberries

Edible flowers (optional)

CRUNCH
Italian bread

Marcona almonds

ACCOUTREMENTS
Balsamic vinegar

Extra-virgin olive oil

SUPPLIES
Cocktail picks or toothpicks

BUILD IT

Prep: Wash and dry all produce. Remove the stems from the strawberries and slice in half. Slice half of the cherry tomatoes in half and the heirloom tomatoes (if using) into wedges. Cut a few of the basil leaves chiffonade, and leave the remaining leaves whole. Make 6 to 8 caprese skewers with whole cherry tomatoes, basil leaves, and balls of mozzarella.

Build: Arrange the **burrata (1)** and a few small piles of **mozzarella (2).** Add piles of **tomatoes (3), strawberries (4),** and **raspberries (5),** mixing and matching the elements in each pile to add dimension. Fold the **salami (6)** and **prosciutto (7),** and tuck them into open spaces. Add 2 to 3 piles of **caprese skewers (8).**

Continue layering mozzarella, tomatoes, and berries—we're going for an "undone," bountiful look! Garnish with small piles of **marcona almonds (9),** whole and chopped **basil (10),** and **edible flowers (11)** (if using).

Serve: Enjoy immediately. Serve with Italian bread, extra-virgin olive oil, and balsamic vinegar on the side.

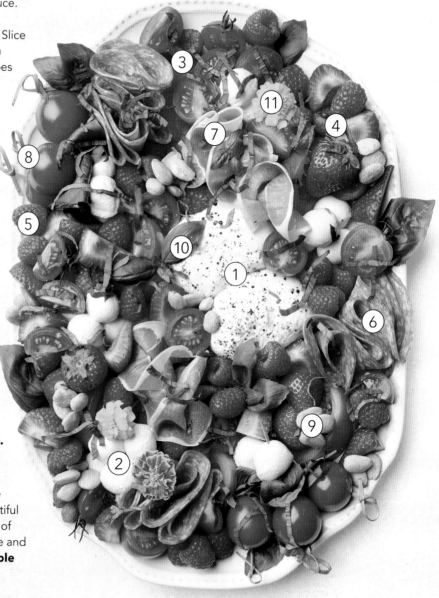

SPOTLIGHT ON FRESH CHEESES: MOZZARELLA & BURRATA

While fresh mozzarella and burrata are available year-round, these two cheeses were *made* for summer. These fresh Italian cheeses both have light and silky textures and mild, milky flavor profiles—and both of these attributes strike the perfect balance with the bright, bold flavors of peak summer produce. They're served cool to preserve their freshness—truly a refreshing approach to cheese during the hot summer.

FRESH MOZZARELLA

What it is: Fresh mozzarella is a stretched curd cheese (pasta filata) with origins in Italy's Campania region. It was originally crafted with milk from local water buffalo and called *mozzarella di bufala*, a style which is still highly sought after and preferred by many for its rich flavor (but is less commonly available due to strict production methods and availability of water buffalo milk). Mozzarella made with cow's milk *(fior di latte)* is much more common today, particularly in the US, and is an equally special and delicious cheese.

What it's like: It's a fresh cheese with a delicate, milky flavor; clean white color; and pillowy, slightly elastic texture that melts in the mouth. As the name implies, fresh mozzarella is not aged or cured. It is intended to be eaten immediately after being made. It's stored in tubs of water or whey to preserve freshness. Mozzarella is available in a variety of sizes, from balls the size of clementines to smaller ones the size of eggs (bocconcini), cherries (ciliegine), and pearls (perline).

How to enjoy it: The beauty of fresh mozzarella is its versatility. It's absolutely *delicious* on its own, but the clean, mild flavor makes it the perfect canvas for simple, flavorful accompaniments. Try it with extra-virgin olive oil, salt, pepper, and Italian bread; in a salad with tomatoes and basil *(insalata caprese)*; or paired with melon, prosciutto, and mint.

BURRATA

What it is: Hailing from the Puglia region of Italy where it originated in the early 1900s, burrata is a cheese made with fresh mozzarella and cream. Burrata can be made with water buffalo milk or cow's milk. Although it looks like and is made with mozzarella, burrata is *not* mozzarella—and the key difference is what's on the inside. Here's a clue: the word *burrata* means "buttered" in Italian.

What it's like: Hidden inside a delicate, fresh mozzarella pouch is a soft, creamy filling of stracciatella cheese—a blend of shredded mozzarella and fresh cream. Slice open the exterior with a knife to reveal the creamy, spreadable insides bursting with decadent, silky texture and heavenly buttery flavor.

How to enjoy it: Don't tell the others, but burrata is hands down my favorite cheese to enjoy during the summer. There's nothing like slicing open that plump mozzarella pouch filled with its cool, creamy, delicious filling and pairing it with the season's best produce (and a glass of chilled rosé). With its luxurious texture and light, buttery flavor, burrata is a great addition to summer salads, pastas, and appetizers.

WINE & CHEESE PAIRINGS

Cheeses vary dramatically in moisture content, fat content, texture, and flavor, while wines vary in acidity, sweetness, body, and structure. What does this mean? Well, that wine and cheese pairings are not a straightforward science! Here are some guidelines to consider when you get started.

- Neither the wine nor the cheese should dominate the other, so select varieties of equal intensity.
- Sharp and aged cheeses pair well with full-bodied wines.
- Bold, sweet, or textured wines stand up well to pungent and funky cheeses.
- Fatty, rich, and soft cheeses demand wines with a higher acidity to cut through the richness.

RED

Hard cheeses, such as aged cheddar, aged Gouda, aged Manchego, Gruyère, and Parmigiano-Reggiano

Blue cheeses, such as Roquefort or Stilton

ROSÉ

Semisoft cheeses, such as Brie, havarti, and Tomme

Fresh cheeses, such as mozzarella and burrata

Semihard cheeses, such as Manchego and cheddar

WHITE

Semihard cheeses, such as mild cheddar, Emmental, and Gouda

Fresh cheeses, such as chèvre and mozzarella

Washed-rind cheeses, such as Taleggio and Époisses

SPARKLING

Soft, rich cheeses, such as Boursin, Brie, burrata, and Camembert

Funky, stinky, or heavy cheeses, such as Gorgonzola or Rush Creek Reserve

ANTIPASTO DINNER BOARD

When it's too darn hot to cook and you'd rather soak up the sun than make a trip to the grocery store, there's only one solution. Say it with me: Cheese board for dinner. The best part about this antipasto board is that you probably already have many of the ingredients in your kitchen—and anything you're missing can be purchased premade from the grocery store olive bar or global foods aisle.

Shopping List

CHEESE
(1) Fresh mozzarella (marinated or plain)
(2) Gorgonzola
(3) Parmigiano-Reggiano (or other hard Italian cheese, such as Asiago)
(4) Robiola

MEAT
(5) Calabrese sopressata
(6) Capicola
(7) Genoa salami
(8) Prosciutto

PRODUCE
(9) Basil
(10) Cherry tomatoes
(9) Rosemary

CRUNCH
(11) Italian bread
(12) Marcona almonds
(13) Taralli crackers

ACCOUTREMENTS
(14) Bruschetta
(15) Marinated artichokes
(16) Olives
(17) Peppadew peppers
(18) Roasted red peppers
(19) Additional antipasto items of choice (optional)

Prep: Slice and toast the bread. Make a salami rose (page 97). Slice the cherry tomatoes in half. Add the olives, artichokes, roasted peppers, and bruschetta to small bowls. **Build:** Arrange the ingredients on the board. **Serve:** Enjoy immediately. Serve with extra bread and crackers on the side.

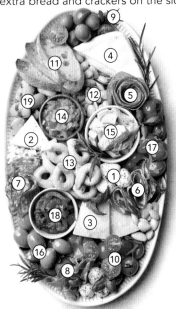

STONE FRUIT SEASON BOARD

Summer is wonderful for so many reasons, and stone fruit is at the top of the list. I can't think of anything better on a hot summer day than a ripe, juicy peach or a bowl of sweet, sun-ripened cherries. These beautiful, decadent fruits are only at their peak for a short window of time, so take full advantage by adding them to salads, desserts, and boards like this one filled with light, creamy cheeses and sweet accoutrements.

Shopping List

CHEESE

(1) Burrata

(2) Marinated chèvre (such as CHEVOO or see recipe on page 93)

(3) Mascarpone

MEAT

(4) Prosciutto

PRODUCE

(5) Apricots

(6) Basil

(7) Cherries

(8) Cherry plums

(9) Nectarines

(10) Peaches

(11) Plumcots

(6) Thyme

CRUNCH

(12) Baguette

(13) Flatbread crackers

(14) Fruit and nut crisps

(15) Marcona almonds

ACCOUTREMENTS

(16) Balsamic glaze

(17) Honey

(18) Peach jam

Prep: Wash, dry, and prep all produce. Slice the baguette. Add the jam, mascarpone, honey, chèvre, and balsamic glaze to small bowls. **Build:** Arrange the ingredients on the board. **Serve:** Enjoy immediately or cover and refrigerate until 20 to 30 minutes before serving.

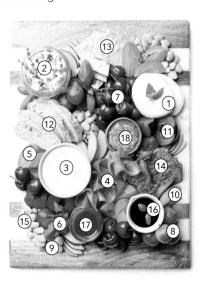

S'MORES DESSERT BOARD

Is there a more quintessential summer dessert than s'mores? They're simple, delicious, and full of nostalgia for summer nights spent around a bonfire. This build-your-own s'mores board offers a smorgasbord of ingredients and toppings that take your humble s'more to the next level. The sky's the limit, so feel free to add your own favorite sweet and salty treats to the mix!

Shopping List

PRODUCE
(1) Raspberries

(2) Strawberries

CRUNCH
(3) Biscoff cookies

(4) Butter waffle cookies

(5) Chocolate-covered pretzels

(6) Cinnamon graham crackers

(7) Honey graham crackers

ACCOUTREMENTS
(8) Caramel chocolates

(9) Chocolate bars

(10) Chocolate-covered nuts

(11) Chocolate morsels or sprinkles

(12) Marshmallows

(13) Peanut butter cups

SUPPLIES
Skewers

Prep: Wash, dry, and prep all produce. Add the chocolate morsels to a small bowl. **Build:** Arrange the ingredients on the board. **Serve:** Enjoy fireside with skewers for roasting the marshmallows.

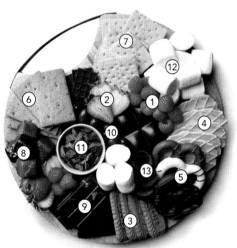

4TH OF JULY BOARD

The 4th of July is one of my favorite holidays—especially when it comes to the food. From the juicy watermelon and sweet corn on the cob to the hot dogs and red, white, and blue desserts, it's one of those holidays with a menu to look forward to. This board is one of my favorite ways to add a twist to the 4th of July menu while staying true to the flavors and colors of the day.

Shopping List

CHEESE
(1) Cheddar
(2) Humboldt Fog
(3) Mozzarella or provolone slices
(4) Pleasant Ridge Reserve

MEAT
(5) Hard salami
(6) Prosciutto

PRODUCE
(7) Blackberries
(7) Blueberries
(8) Cherries

(9) Raspberries
(10) Strawberries
(11) Watermelon

CRUNCH
(12) Flatbread crackers
(13) Pita bread
(14) Star-shaped crackers or cookies

ACCOUTREMENTS
(15) Cherry jam
(16) Honey

SUPPLIES
Star cookie cutter

For little hands: Have the kids use the cookie cutter to create cutouts of the mozzarella, pita, and watermelon. **Prep:** Wash, dry, and prep all produce. Thinly slice the salami, cheddar, and Pleasant Ridge Reserve. Add the jam and honey to small bowls. **Build:** Arrange the ingredients on the board. **Serve:** Enjoy immediately or cover and refrigerate until 20 to 30 minutes before serving.

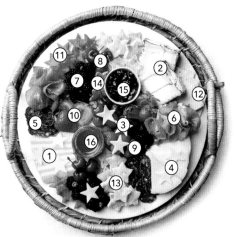

FARMERS MARKET BOARD

One of my favorite summer rituals is a Saturday morning spent strolling through the farmers market: coffee in one hand, market bag in the other. I love stocking up on the season's best produce (hello, peak tomato season) and discovering new vendors and their artisanal wares. The farmers market is the perfect place to stock up on some really special items for a cheese board—from beautiful fruits and vegetables and locally crafted cheeses to homemade jams and freshly baked bread.

Shopping List

CHEESE
(1) Feta (marinated or plain)
(2) Herb chèvre
(3) Herb havarti or cheddar

MEAT
(4) Prosciutto

PRODUCE
(5) Blackberries
(6) Cherries
(7) Figs
(8) Grapes
(9) Lavender
(9) Oregano
(10) Red pears
(9) Thyme

CRUNCH
(11) Baguette
(12) Marcona almonds

ACCOUTREMENTS
(13) Honeycomb
(13) Local honey
Jam (optional)

Prep: Wash, dry, and prep all produce. Cut the havarti into thin rectangular pieces. Slice or tear the baguette. Add the honey, feta, and jam (if using) to small bowls. **Build:** Arrange the ingredients on the board. **Serve:** Enjoy immediately or cover and refrigerate until 20 to 30 minutes before serving.

Fall

Your Fall
Pantry

"Autumn carries more gold in its pocket than all the other seasons." –John Bishop
It's natural to assume that the gold John Bishop refers to is the color of fall foliage, but I like to think he's describing other ways in which this season is richer than the others: from its bountiful harvests to its celebrations of gratitude and traditions of gathering.

Whether you're cramming friends into a tiny apartment for Friendsgiving or gathered with family around a kitchen island filled with appetizers, this season was made for creating memories and celebrating traditions. This final chapter is filled with ideas for boards to gather around all season long. But before we dive in, let's explore our fall pantry:

The Produce:
Apples
Blackberries
Black grapes
Cranberries
Figs
Golden berries
Gourds and pumpkins
Pears
Persimmons
Pomegranates
Red grapes

The Cheeses:
Aged Gouda
BellaVitano
Brie
Camembert
Chimay
Clothbound cheddar
Cranberry chèvre
Cranberry Wensleydale
Double-Cream Cremont
Emmental
Fromager d'Affinois
Gruyère
Harbison
Mimolette
Parmigiano-Reggiano
Pleasant Ridge Reserve
Rogue River Blue
Roquefort
Rush Creek Reserve
Taleggio
Vintage cheddar

The Accoutrements:
Apple jam
Cornichons
Dried cranberries
Dried persimmons
Fig and olive crisps
Fig jam
Grainy mustard
Honey
Olives
Pear mostarda
Pepitas
Roasted nuts
Rustic crackers
Spiced pear jam
Spiced pecans

FALL PAIRINGS BOARD

Of all the seasons, fall is perhaps the one most distinctly defined by its flavors. From pumpkin spice and apple cider to the turkey and sweet potatoes at Thanksgiving dinner, our favorite quintessential fall foods are beloved for their warm, complex, and savory flavors—not to mention their rich colors and comforting aromas. With an abundance of fall flavors to mix and match and an array of gorgeous colors, this board is a feast for the senses and a must-have for the season's gatherings.

Shopping List

CHEESE
Cabot Clothbound Cheddar
Fromager d'Affinois
Roquefort

MEAT
Hard salami
Prosciutto

PRODUCE
Blackberries
Bosc pears
Persimmons (fresh or dried)
Red grapes
Rosemary
Sage

CRUNCH
Fig and olive crisps
Marcona almonds
Spiced pecans
Flatbread crackers (optional)

ACCOUTREMENTS
Fig jam
Grainy mustard
Honey (optional)

BUILD IT

Prep: Wash and dry all produce. Cut the pears, persimmons, and salami into thin slices. Cut the pomegranate into small segments, leaving 3 to 4 segments whole and removing the arils from the rest. Use the tip of a knife to break off bite-sized pieces of cheddar and Roquefort. Spoon the jam, mustard, and honey (if using) into small bowls.

Build: Arrange the **Cabot Clothbound Cheddar (1)**, **Fromager d'Affinois (2)**, and **Roquefort (3)** near the edges of the board. Place the bowls of **jam (4)**, **mustard (5)**, and honey (if using). Create a few piles each of **grapes (6)** and **blackberries (7)**, and add neat stacks of **pears (8)** and **persimmons (9)**.

Fold the **prosciutto (10)** and tuck it into an open space. Build a layered pile of **salami (11)**. Arrange a stack of **crisps (12)**. Fill in any gaps with **marcona almonds (13)** and **spiced pecans (14)**. Garnish with **rosemary** and **sage (15)**.

Serve: Enjoy immediately or cover and refrigerate until 20 to 30 minutes before serving.

Enjoy this bountiful arrangement chock-full of fall flavors and delicious pairing possibilities.

| PAIRINGS | The bold flavors and decadent textures of these cheeses are perfectly paired with seasonal produce and sweet and savory accoutrements. There are many ways to mix and match, but here are a few of my favorite combinations. |

FROMAGER D'AFFINOIS

Blackberries

Fig and olive
crisps

Fig jam

Prosciutto

Spiced
pecans

CABOT CLOTHBOUND CHEDDAR

Fig and olive
crisps

Grainy mustard

Prosciutto

Red grapes

Salami

ROQUEFORT

Bosc pears

Fig and olive
crisps

Grainy mustard

Persimmons

Prosciutto

FALL GATHERINGS BOARD

Beyond the fun holidays, cozy sweaters, and warm beverages that define the months of September through November, the season's tradition of gathering with friends and family is really what makes fall so special.

The crisp, cool air and colorful foliage create the perfect setting for cozy evenings spent huddled around a bonfire or seated around the dinner table. This bountiful, flavorful board is one you'll want to gather around all season long, whether you're heading to a spontaneous backyard get-together or hosting a meticulously planned dinner party.

Shopping List

CHEESE
Aged Gouda
Brie
Double-Cream Cremont
Pleasant Ridge Reserve

MEAT
Hard salami
Prosciutto

PRODUCE
Blackberries
Persimmons (fresh or dried)
Pomegranate
Red Anjou pears
Red grapes
Rosemary
Thyme

CRUNCH
Fig and olive crisps
Flatbread crackers
Marcona almonds
Pepitas

ACCOUTREMENTS
Cornichons
Fig jam
Honey
Pear mostarda (or other savory spread, such as caramelized onion jam)

BUILD IT

Prep: Wash and dry all produce. Cut the pears, persimmons, and salami into thin slices. Cut the pomegranate into small segments. Slice the Pleasant Ridge Reserve into thin rectangular pieces. Use the tip of a knife to break off bite-sized pieces of Gouda. Add the jams and honey to small bowls.

Build: Arrange the **aged Gouda (1), Brie (2), Pleasant Ridge Reserve (3),** and **Double-Cream Cremont (4)** near the edges of the board, and place the small bowls of **fig jam (5), pear mostarda (6),** and **honey (7).** Build 2 to 3 piles each of **grapes (8), blackberries (9),** and **cornichons (10).**

Fold and arrange the **prosciutto (11).** Build a layered pile of the sliced **salami (12).** Create stacked arrangements of **crackers (13)** and **crisps (14).** Add the segments of **pomegranate (15)** and small stacks of **sliced pear (16)** and **persimmon (17)** to open spaces. Fill in any remaining gaps with **marcona almonds (18)** and **pepitas (19).** Garnish with **rosemary** and **thyme (20)** and **pomegranate arils (21).**

Serve: Enjoy immediately or cover and refrigerate until 20 to 30 minutes before serving.

Gather / gath·er / verb: come together; assemble.

STYLING GUIDE: FALL ENTERTAINING

When you're hosting a gathering, any opportunity to shorten your to-do list is a blessing. A beautifully styled cheese board is your secret to checking off the appetizers and table decor from your list.

Here are some tips for styling a show-stopping board that pulls double duty as a feast for the eyes *and* the taste buds.

Choose your canvas. A large board, tray, platter, or even a cake stand will do. Bonus if you can find one with "feet" or a pedestal to give it some height off the table or countertop.

Build your color story. Layer seasonal fruit to "paint" the board with rich, autumn colors. For an extra elevated look, garnish with gourds, pomegranates, or persimmons.

Bring it to life. Fill up your board to the edges, piling items high and close for a full, bountiful look. Garnish with herbs to bring the board to life with fresh color and fragrance.

OKTOBERFEST BOARD

There's no doubt that Oktoberfest is known for beer, but when I think of the iconic celebration, my first thought is pretzels. That's right, pretzels. Soft pretzels, crispy pretzels, strings of mini pretzels worn like necklaces—you get the idea.

Inspired by my pretzel-filled daydreams of checking Oktoberfest off my bucket list, the ingredients on this board will transport you to the beer garden–filled streets of Munich. Lederhosen not required.

Shopping List

CHEESE
Beer Cheese Dip
 (page 165)
Butterkäse
Cambozola
Smoked Gouda

MEAT
German sausage

PRODUCE
Blackberries
Red grapes
Rosemary

CRUNCH
Mixed nuts
Pretzel twists
Soft pretzels

ACCOUTREMENTS
Cornichons
Dijon mustard
Grainy mustard
Green olives

BUILD IT

Prep: Wash and dry all produce. Bake the soft pretzels according to the package instructions. Slice the sausage into bite-sized pieces. Make the Beer Cheese Dip (page 165), and add to a small bowl. Slice the Butterkäse into thin rectangular pieces. Slice a few thin wedges of smoked Gouda, leaving the rest of the wheel whole. Add the mustards to small bowls.

Build: Arrange the **Butterkäse (1), Cambozola (2),** and **smoked Gouda (3)** near the edges of the board. Place the bowls of **grainy mustard (4), Dijon mustard (5),** and **Beer Cheese Dip (6).** Arrange the **soft pretzels (7)** and **German sausage (8),** and build piles of **pretzel twists (9).** Add a few small piles each of **blackberries (10)** and **grapes (11).** Repeat with **cornichons (12)** and **olives (13).** Fill in any gaps with **mixed nuts (14).** Garnish with **rosemary (15).**

Serve: Enjoy immediately.

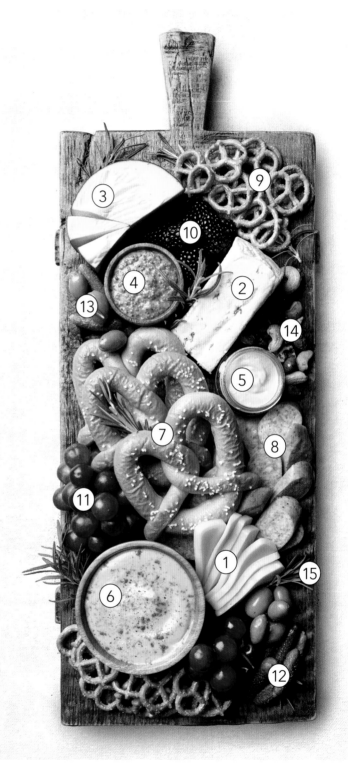

BEER CHEESE DIP

Few things warm the soul on a crisp fall day better than a warm, cheesy dip. This flavorful, melty beer cheese dip fits the bill and is the perfect accompaniment for salty, crunchy pretzels. It's best enjoyed al fresco at an Oktoberfest celebration or tailgate party with a cold beverage in hand.

MAKES: 8 servings
TOTAL TIME: 20 minutes

2 cups sharp cheddar cheese (or for a more complex flavor, use a combination of smoked Gouda or Gruyère cheese; avoid preshredded cheese)

4 tbsp unsalted butter
¼ cup all-purpose flour
1 cup whole milk
1 cup beer (such as a German wheat beer)
2 tsp Worcestershire sauce

½ tsp Dijon or spicy brown mustard
½ tsp garlic powder
¼ tsp smoked paprika
¼ tsp salt
¼ tsp freshly ground black pepper

1. Shred the cheese using a box grater.

2. In a small saucepan, melt the butter over medium-high heat. To make a roux, add the flour and whisk to combine until it becomes a thick paste.

3. Slowly pour in the milk and whisk until thickened, about 2 minutes.

4. Add the beer and Worcestershire sauce, and whisk until smooth and thickened, about 5 minutes.

5. Add the mustard, garlic powder, paprika, salt, and pepper. Stir to combine.

6. Remove the pot from the heat and add the shredded cheese. Stir until the cheese is all melted and the mixture is smooth and creamy.

7. Serve warm as a dipping sauce.

Pretzels and a variety of savory dips add a flavorful twist to an assortment of bold German cheeses.

BEER & CHEESE PAIRINGS

We all know that wine and cheese are like two peas in a pod, but the carbonation and complex flavors of a cold beer make it a good friend to cheese, too! Take the time to relish the flavors together and notice how they harmonize and sometimes even bring out new flavors you hadn't noticed. Here are some general tips to keep in mind, but as always, pairings are personal, so feel free to experiment with your own combinations!

- You don't want your beer to stifle the cheese, so pair blander cheeses with milder beers.
- Strong and hoppy beers complement mature and full-bodied cheeses.
- Heavy beers pair nicely with rich and buttery cheeses, and especially sharp cheeses.
- Prominently fruity beers in general go well with any type of cheese.

LAGER & PILSNER
Brie
Chèvre
Havarti
Mild cheddar

HEFEWEIZEN
Butterkäse
Chèvre
Feta
Fresh mozzarella
Gouda

PALE ALE, IPA, AMBER ALE, & BROWN ALE

Aged and English cheddars

Aged Gouda

Camembert

Washed-rind cheeses, such as Taleggio or Patacabra

STOUT & PORTER

Aged Gouda

Beaufort

Blue cheeses, such as Stilton, Roquefort, and Point Reyes Blue

Comté

Coupole

Parmigiano-Reggiano

GAME DAY SNACK BOARD

Fall and football season go hand-in-hand, and while football is certainly not my forte, even I can't deny the allure of a game-day gathering on a gorgeous, crisp fall afternoon. Game-day snacks are some of my favorites to make and enjoy, especially when they're served up on a colorful, show-stopping board!

Let's take a look at the play-by-play of this game-day snack board that's a guaranteed touchdown, whether you're watching games at home or heading to a tailgate.

Shopping List

CHEESE
Dill or chipotle havarti
Goat Cheese Buffalo Dip
(page 171)
Pepper Jack

MEAT
Calabrese salami
Prosciutto

PRODUCE
Carrots
Celery
Parsley
Snap peas

CRUNCH
Pecans
Pistachios
Potato chips
Pretzels

SNACKS
Meatballs
Mozzarella sticks
Pigs in a blanket
Wings (flavor of choice)
Other appetizers of choice
(optional; such as
jalapeño poppers, potato
skins, tater tots, etc.)

ACCOUTREMENTS
Cornichons
Dips and condiments of
choice (2–3 varieties, such
as veggie dip, chip dip,
hummus, marinara sauce,
blue cheese, ranch, etc.)
Olives
Pickled jalapeño slices

BUILD IT

Prep: Wash and dry all produce. Slice the carrots and celery into thin, snackable sticks. Make the Goat Cheese Buffalo Dip (page 171). Slice the havarti and pepper Jack into thin rectangular pieces. Add the dips and condiments to small bowls or ramekins. Heat the mozzarella sticks, meatballs, pigs in a blanket, and wings according to the package instructions.

Build: Set the foundation with the **dips and condiments (1)**, and reserve small sections for the foods with which the dips pair. Reserve space for the Goat Cheese Buffalo Dip.

Neatly arrange the **carrots (2), celery (2)**, and **snap peas (3)** around the appropriate dip. Place the **havarti (4)** and **pepper Jack (5).** Fold and place the **salami (6)** and **prosciutto (7).** Add piles of **pistachios (8), pecans (9), cornichons (10)**, and **olives (11).** Add the **Goat Cheese Buffalo Dip (12).** Place the **mozzarella sticks (13), meatballs (14), pigs in a blanket (15)**, and **wings (16)** in the reserved spaces near their coordinating dips. Build piles of **chips (17)** and **pretzels (18)** around the buffalo dip. Garnish with **parsley (19)** and **jalapeño slices (20).**

Serve: Enjoy with extra crackers and chips on the side. If you'll be transporting the board to a party or tailgate, lay a few sheets of aluminum foil on your workspace before you begin building (make sure the edges of the foil extend well past the edges of the board), and place the empty board or tray on top. When you're done building your masterpiece, bring the edges of the fold up and over the top of the board and seal.

Snack boards are as fun to shop for as they are to create! Choose your favorite snacks, dips, and apps, and elevate them with a bountiful, colorful arrangement.

GOAT CHEESE BUFFALO DIP

Everyone's favorite buffalo dip gets a zippy, creamy upgrade thanks to the addition of fresh goat cheese. It's a simple upgrade that takes this game day classic from delicious to simply irresistible.

MAKES: 4–6 servings

TOTAL TIME: 35 minutes

5 oz (140g) plain fresh goat cheese, room temperature	½ cup blue cheese crumbles
8 oz (225g) cream cheese, room temperature	½ cup shredded mozzarella, plus more for topping
½ cup plain Greek yogurt	¼ cup shredded cheddar, plus more for topping
1 tbsp lemon juice	Chives, for garnish
½ cup Frank's RedHot	

1. Preheat the oven to 350°F (180°C).

2. In a medium bowl or food processor, beat together the goat cheese and cream cheese. Once well combined, mix in the Greek yogurt and lemon juice.

3. Add the Frank's RedHot, blue cheese crumbles, and shredded mozzarella. Mix to combine. The mixture will look runny, but it will firm up as it bakes.

4. Transfer the mixture to a baking dish and top with extra shredded mozzarella and cheddar.

5. Bake for 20 minutes, or until the dip is bubbly and the top is golden brown.

6. Remove from the oven and top with sliced chives. Allow to cool for 10 minutes.

7. Serve with your favorite chips, crackers, or veggies.

AFTER SCHOOL SNACK BOARD

Most days, an after school snack is a granola bar in the back seat on the way to soccer practice—a practical necessity—but on those rare days when there are no activities to rush to or last-minute projects to complete, an after school snack can be an opportunity to gather around the table and reconnect. On those days, however few and far between, add a special twist to snack time with a kid-friendly cheese board filled with ingredients for the kids to mix and match as they build their own bites and explore new flavor combinations.

Shopping List

CHEESE
Babybel Cheese
Mild cheddar
Mozzarella string cheese
Provolone slices

MEAT
Sliced Genoa salami
Sliced turkey breast

PRODUCE
Blackberries
Blueberries
Clementines
Red grapes
Strawberries

CRUNCH
Animal crackers
Graham crackers
Pretzel twists
Ritz crackers
Trail mix
Yogurt-covered pretzels

ACCOUTREMENTS
Fruit snacks
Goldfish
Gummy candy
Hummus
Peanut butter

SUPPLIES
Cocktail picks or
 toothpicks
Small cookie cutters

BUILD IT

For little hands: Enlist little helpers to prepare each of the Kid-Friendly Bites (page 175). Then have the kids decide where to place pops of color while assembling!

Prep: Wash and dry all produce. Slice the strawberries in half. Peel and segment the clementines. Add the peanut butter, trail mix, and hummus to small bowls. Cut the Babybels in half.

Build: Arrange the **Turkey & Cheese Skewers (1), Mozzarella Bites (2),** and **Babybels (3).** Place the bowls of **peanut butter (4), trail mix (5),** and **hummus (6).** Add piles of **grapes (7), strawberries (8), blueberries (9),** and **clementines (10).**

Place the **Ritz crackers (11), graham crackers (12), pretzel twists (13),** and **yogurt-covered pretzels (14)** near the bowls of peanut butter and hummus for easy dipping. Build piles of **animal crackers (15), Goldfish (16), fruit snacks (17),** and **gummy candy (18).** Garnish with the **Cheese Cut-Outs (19).**

Serve: Enjoy immediately or cover and refrigerate until 20 to 30 minutes before serving.

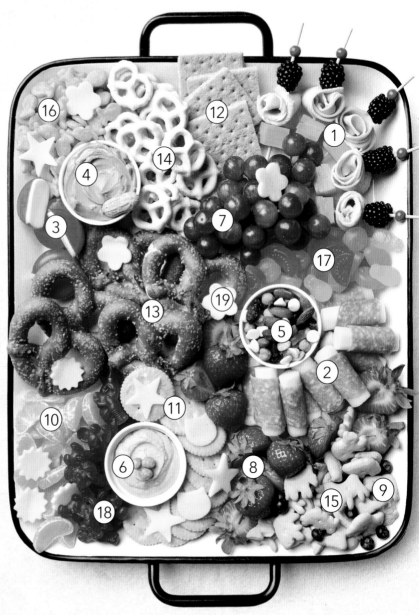

Building the board is half the fun, so let everyone play along as you choose ingredients and decide how to arrange your beautiful, colorful board.

STYLING TIPS: KID-FRIENDLY BITES

Grab your little helpers and create these simple ready-to-eat bites that make for simple snacking and add a fun sensory element to your board.

1. **Turkey & Cheddar Skewers:** To each skewer, add a blackberry, slice of turkey breast, and bite of cheddar cheese.
2. **Mozzarella Bites:** Cut the string cheeses and slices of Genoa salami in half. Wrap the salami around the mozzarella.
3. **Cheese Cutouts:** Use a variety of small cookie cutters to cut shapes from the provolone slices.

MOVIE NIGHT BOARD

Every good movie night needs snacks—and if you ask me, the snacks are *almost* more important than the movie. Take movie night from good to great by gathering everyone's favorite movie theater candy, popcorn, and salty snacks. Bonus points if the shapes, colors, and snacks match the movie theme. Build a colorful, sweet, and salty board to graze on from the opening scene to the closing credits.

Shopping List

CHEESE
(1) Gouda
(2) Havarti
(3) Sharp cheddar

MEAT
(4) Genoa salami

PRODUCE
(5) Apples
(6) Carrots
(7) Celery
(8) Red grapes

ACCOUTREMENTS
(9) Hummus
(10) Peanut butter

CRUNCH
(11) Cheddar twists
(12) Chocolate chip cookies
(13) Oreos
(14) Peanut butter–filled pretzels
(15) Popcorn (2 varieties)
(16) Pretzel twists
(17) Trail mix

CANDY
(18) Gummy candy
(19) Peanut butter cups
(20) Red Hots
(21) Twizzlers
Other candies of choice (optional)

Prep: Wash, dry, and prep all produce. Then slice the cheeses into thin pieces. **Build:** Arrange the ingredients on the board. **Serve:** Enjoy immediately.

AROUND THE
APPLE SPICE BOARD

Don't tell the pumpkins, but apples are the true heroes of fall. Crisp and tangy, juicy and sweet, apples are the perfect companion to sweet and savory items alike. This board is an apple lover's dream with its variety of apples to pair with cheeses, charcuterie, and fun accoutrements for delicious bites that are bursting with fall flavor.

Shopping List

CHEESE

(1) Aged Gouda

(2) Brie

(3) Cinnamon toscano (or plain toscano or BellaVitano)

(4) Sharp white cheddar

MEAT

(5) Applewood smoked salami

PRODUCE

(6) Gala apple

(7) Granny Smith apple

(8) Honeycrisp apple

CRUNCH

(9) Cheddar twists

(10) Cinnamon graham crackers

(11) Dried apples

(12) Maple cookies

(13) Spiced pecans

(14) Taralli crackers

ACCOUTREMENTS

(15) Apple cider jam

(16) Honey

EXTRAS

(17) Cinnamon sticks

Prep: Wash, dry, and prep all produce. Thinly slice the Brie and cheddar. Use the tip of a knife to break off bite-sized pieces of Gouda and toscano. Add the jam and honey to small bowls. **Build:** Arrange the ingredients on the board. **Serve:** Enjoy immediately.

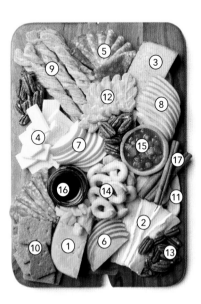

CHARSPOOKERIE BOARD

AROUND THE

From the clever costumes and spooky decor to the scary movies and trick-or-treat traditions, Halloween takes the cake as my favorite holiday. As a self-proclaimed ghostess with the mostest, I've learned a thing or two about hosting a delightfully spooky and frighteningly creative gathering. The most requested recipe in my book of spells? A spooky board with a dark and moody color palette and eye-catching ingredients that set the tone for a wickedly elegant evening.

Shopping List

CHEESE

(1) Gorgonzola Piccante

(2) Humboldt Fog (classic or Chipotle Cacao Remix)

(3) La Tur (or Vermont Creamery's Coupole)

(4) Mimolette

MEAT

(5) Bresaola

(6) Salami secchi

PRODUCE

(7) Blackberries

(8) Figs (fresh or dried)

(9) Thomcord or black grapes

Blood oranges (optional)

CRUNCH

(10) Fig and olive crisps

(11) Spiced pecans

ACCOUTREMENTS

(12) Dark chocolate

(13) Dried citrus

(14) Dried cranberries

(15) Honeycomb

(16) Sour cherry jam

Prep: Wash, dry, and prep all produce. Thinly slice the salami. Add the jam to a small bowl.

Build: Arrange the ingredients on the board.

Serve: Enjoy immediately or cover and refrigerate until 20 to 30 minutes before serving.

THANKSGIVING BOARD

The Thanksgiving menu is sacred. You probably have your own family recipes and traditions—it's a big part of what makes the holiday so special. But there's always room for new traditions, and in recent years, a cheese board has become an important addition to my family's Thanksgiving menu. Not only is a board a great solution for a simplified appetizer menu, it's also a surefire way to get the celebration started as family gathers around to catch up and enjoy delicious bites before the main event.

Shopping List

CHEESE
(1) Cranberry chèvre
(2) Gruyère
(3) Harbison
(4) Port Salut

MEAT
(5) Prosciutto
(6) Sopressata

PRODUCE
(7) Bosc pears
(8) Golden berries
(9) Persimmons (fresh or dried)
(10) Pomegranate
(11) Raspberries

(12) Red grapes
(13) Rosemary
(13) Sage
(13) Thyme

CRUNCH
(14) Fig and olive crisps
(15) Flatbread crackers
(16) Marcona almonds
(17) Pepitas

ACCOUTREMENTS
(18) Fig jam
(19) Honey
(20) Honeycomb

Prep: Wash, dry, and prep all produce. Slice the Gruyère into thin pieces. Slice off the top rind of the Harbison. Add the jam and honey to small bowls. **Build:** Arrange the ingredients on the board. **Serve:** Enjoy immediately or cover and refrigerate until 20 to 30 minutes before serving.

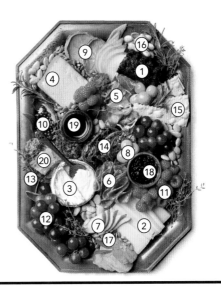

FRIENDSGIVING BOARD

I've always loved the idea of a secondary celebration to the family-centered Thanksgiving holiday—after all, Thanksgiving is all about gathering in gratitude with the people we care about most. This board is inspired by one I made for a Friendsgiving gathering in 2018—the board that sparked the idea to build a community around my passion for gathering around beautiful boards and the reason that you're holding this book in your hands.

Shopping List

CHEESE

(1) Aged Gouda
(2) Boursin
(3) Cranberry chèvre
(4) English cheddar
(5) Triple-crème cheese

MEAT

(6) Capicola
(7) Genoa salami
(8) Hard sopressata
(9) Prosciutto

PRODUCE

(10) Blackberries
(11) Pomegranate
(12) Red grapes

(13) Rosemary
(13) Sage
Pears (optional)

CRUNCH

(14) Fig and olive crisps
(15) Flatbread crackers
(16) Marcona almonds
(17) Mini toasts
(18) Pepitas
(19) Walnuts

ACCOUTREMENTS

(20) Castelvetrano olives
(21) Fig jam
(22) Honey

Prep: Wash, dry, and prep all produce. Thinly slice the sopressata. Cut the cheddar into bite-sized pieces. Use the tip of a knife to break off bite-sized pieces of Gouda. Add the jam, honey, and almonds to small bowls.
Build: Arrange the ingredients on the board.
Serve: Enjoy immediately or cover and refrigerate until 20 to 30 minutes before serving.

Index

About the Author

Emily Delaney is the founder of *Cheese Board Queen*, a community inspired by her passion for bringing people together around beautiful boards. Whether she's breaking down the steps of a stunning arrangement, sharing expert flavor-pairing tips, or fostering community through workshops, Emily's mission is to take the guesswork out of making delicious boards for all of life's occasions. Born and raised in the Midwest, she resides in Chicago.

Acknowledgments

Simply put, it takes a village, and I'd like to express my gratitude to the members of mine. First and foremost, to my parents, Pam and Darin Delaney, who made the kitchen the heart of our home—a place to grow, gather, and love. Thank you for your wisdom and guidance and for always encouraging me to follow my dreams. To my brother, Nick Delaney, whose wit and sense of humor are second only to his kindness and unwavering support. To my fiancé, Nick Watt, your endless supply of positivity and encouragement is a gift I will cherish forever. Thank you for being my biggest fan. To my friends new and old, near and far, who help me to see the best in myself and inspire me to take on new challenges. Here's to many more evenings spent gathered around a board. To the talented and courageous small business owners and culinary artists who are the backbone of the cheese and artisanal food world. Thank you for sharing your gifts with the world and for allowing me to feature them on these pages. And finally, to the *Cheese Board Queen* community, whose creativity and kindness inspire me daily. Thank you for joining me on this journey. To the incredible team at DK Publishing and everyone who helped bring my vision for this book to life. Special thanks to Alexandra Andrzejewski, Becky Batchelor, Ashley Brooks, and Daniel Showalter.

lp Blossom Applewood Smoked Salami Asiago Bresaola Brie Boursin Burra

noa Salami German Sausage Gorgonzola Gouda Halloumi Harbison Havarti J

rmano Pepper Jack Pepperoni Port Salut Prosciutto Ricotta Roquefort Salami S

oked Salami Asiago Bresaola Brie Boursin Burrata Calabrese Sopressata

usage Gorgonzola Gouda Halloumi Harbison Havarti Humboldt Fog Manc

ck Pepperoni Port Salut Prosciutto Ricotta Roquefort Salami Secchi Sopressata

siago Bresaola Brie Boursin Burrata Calabrese Sopressata Camembert Capico

uda Halloumi Harbison Havarti Humboldt Fog Manchego Mimolette Moz

lut Prosciutto Ricotta Roquefort Salami Secchi Sopressata Stilton Swiss Talegg

rie Boursin Burrata Calabrese Sopressata Camembert Capicola Cheddar Choriz

arbison Havarti Humboldt Fog Manchego Mimolette Mozzarella P'tit Basqu

cotta Roquefort Salami Secchi Sopressata Stilton Swiss Taleggio Truffle Salam

urrata Calabrese Sopressata Camembert Capicola Cheddar Chorizo Feta Fromo